W9-BEP-251

Understanding
World History

The
Holocaust

Charles George and Linda George

Bruno Leone
Series Consultant

ReferencePoint
Press®

San Diego, CA

© 2012 ReferencePoint Press, Inc.
Printed in the United States

For more information, contact:
ReferencePoint Press, Inc.
PO Box 27779
San Diego, CA 92198
www.ReferencePointPress.com

LIBRARY OF CONGRESS CATALOGING-IN-PUBLICATION DATA

George, Charles, 1949–
  The Holocaust : part of the understanding world history series / by Charles George and Linda George.
    p. cm. — (Understanding world history)
  Includes bibliographical references and index.
  ISBN-13: 978-1-60152-155-2 (hardback)
  ISBN-10: 1-60152-155-3 (hardback)
  1. Holocaust, Jewish (1939–1945)—Juvenile literature. I. George, Linda. II. Title.
  D804.34.G46 2010
  940.53'18—dc22

                                                            2010045684

Contents

Foreword

When the Puritans first emigrated from England to America in 1630, they believed that their journey was blessed by a covenant between themselves and God. By the terms of that covenant they agreed to establish a community in the New World dedicated to what they believed was the true Christian faith. God, in turn, would reward their fidelity by making certain that they and their descendants would always experience his protection and enjoy material prosperity. Moreover, the Lord guaranteed that their land would be seen as a shining beacon—or in their words, a "city upon a hill,"—which the rest of the world would view with admiration and respect. By embracing this notion that God could and would shower his favor and special blessings upon them, the Puritans were adopting the providential philosophy of history—meaning that history is the unfolding of a plan established or guided by a higher intelligence.

The concept of intercession by a divine power is only one of many explanations of the driving forces of world history. Historians and philosophers alike have subscribed to numerous other ideas. For example, the ancient Greeks and Romans argued that history is cyclical. Nations and civilizations, according to these ancients of the Western world, rise and fall in unpredictable cycles; the only certainty is that these cycles will persist throughout an endless future. The German historian Oswald Spengler (1880–1936) echoed the ancients to some degree in his controversial study *The Decline of the West.* Spengler asserted that all civilizations inevitably pass through stages comparable to the life span of a person: childhood, youth, adulthood, old age, and, eventually, death. As the title of his work implies, Western civilization is currently entering its final stage.

Joining those who see purpose and direction in history are thinkers who completely reject the idea of meaning or certainty. Rather, they reason that since there are far too many random and unseen factors at work on the earth, historians would be unwise to endorse historical predictability of any type. Warfare (both nuclear and conventional), plagues, earthquakes, tsunamis, meteor showers, and other catastrophic world-changing events have loomed large throughout history and prehistory. In his essay "A Free Man's Worship," philosopher and mathematician Bertrand Russell (1872–1970) supported this argument, which many refer to as the nihilist or chaos theory of history. According to Russell, history follows no preordained path. Rather, the earth itself and all life on earth resulted from, as Russell describes it, an "accidental collocation of atoms." Based on this premise, he pessimistically concluded that all human achievement will eventually be "buried beneath the debris of a universe in ruins."

Whether history does or does not have an underlying purpose, historians, journalists, and countless others have nonetheless left behind a record of human activity tracing back nearly 6,000 years. From the dawn of the great ancient Near Eastern civilizations of Mesopotamia and Egypt to the modern economic and military behemoths China and the United States, humanity's deeds and misdeeds have been and continue to be monitored and recorded. The distinguished British scholar Arnold Toynbee (1889–1975), in his widely acclaimed 12-volume work entitled *A Study of History*, studied 21 different civilizations that have passed through history's pages. He noted with certainty that others would follow.

In the final analysis, the academic and journalistic worlds mostly regard history as a record and explanation of past events. From a more practical perspective, history represents a sequence of building blocks—cultural, technological, military, and political—ready to be utilized and enhanced or maligned and perverted by the present. What that means is that all societies—whether advanced civilizations or preliterate tribal cultures—leave a legacy for succeeding generations to either embrace or disregard.

Recognizing the richness and fullness of history, the ReferencePoint Press Understanding World History series fosters an evaluation and interpretation of history and its influence on later generations. Each volume in the series approaches its subject chronologically and topically, with specific focus on nations, periods, or pivotal events. Primary and secondary source quotations are included, along with complete source notes and suggestions for further research.

Moreover, the series reflects the truism that the key to understanding the present frequently lies in the past. With that in mind, each series title concludes with a legacy chapter that highlights the bonds between past and present and, more important, demonstrates that world history is a continuum of peoples and ideas, sometimes hidden but there nonetheless, waiting to be discovered by those who choose to look.

Important Events of the Holocaust

1543
Martin Luther pens *On the Jews and Their Lies.*

1939
Nazi invasion of Poland sparks World War II; mass murder of Jews begins.

1925
Publication of Hitler's anti-Semitic *Mein Kampf.*

1920
Beginnings of the Nazi Party in Germany.

1900	1910	1920	1930

1889
Birth of Adolf Hitler.

1933
Hitler becomes chancellor of Germany; first concentration camp built at Dachau.

1935
Passage of anti-Jewish Nuremberg Laws.

1938
Kristallnacht, the Night of Broken Glass.

1940
Warsaw ghetto established; Auschwitz constructed.

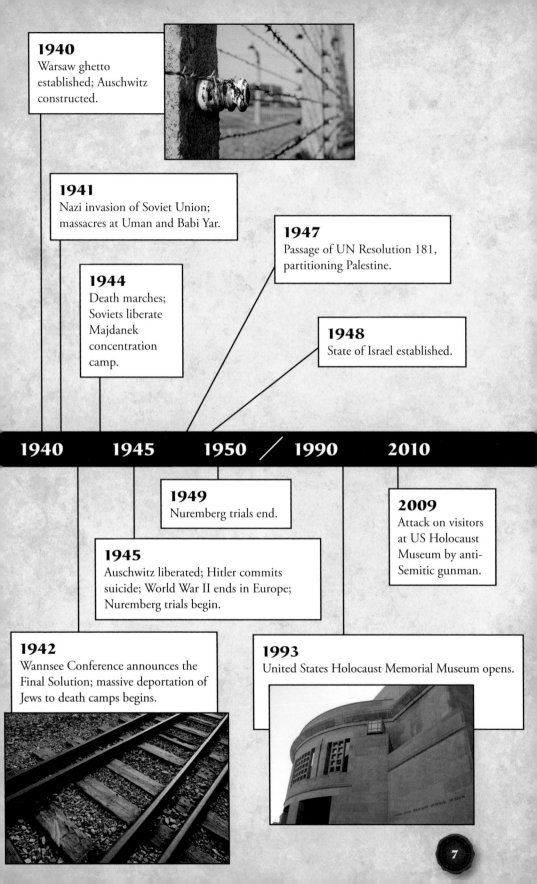

1941
Nazi invasion of Soviet Union; massacres at Uman and Babi Yar.

1947
Passage of UN Resolution 181, partitioning Palestine.

1944
Death marches; Soviets liberate Majdanek concentration camp.

1948
State of Israel established.

| 1940 | 1945 | 1950 / 1990 | 2010 |

1949
Nuremberg trials end.

2009
Attack on visitors at US Holocaust Museum by anti-Semitic gunman.

1945
Auschwitz liberated; Hitler commits suicide; World War II ends in Europe; Nuremberg trials begin.

1942
Wannsee Conference announces the Final Solution; massive deportation of Jews to death camps begins.

1993
United States Holocaust Memorial Museum opens.

The Defining Characteristics of the Holocaust

Elie Wiesel—author, lecturer, Holocaust survivor, and winner of the 1986 Nobel Peace Prize—was 15 years old when officials of Nazi Germany deported him and his family from their homeland in 1944. The Nazis, by that time, had invaded and taken control of Romania, along with most of Europe. On May 16, 1944, the Wiesels, along with hundreds of other Jewish families, were loaded into railroad freight cars in Sighet, Transylvania (northwestern Romania), to be hauled to Auschwitz, a Nazi concentration camp in southwestern Poland. They had committed no crime. They were no threat to the government. They were simply Jews, and Nazis believed all Jews should be eliminated.

Wiesel was one of only three members of his extended family to survive the camps that had been built for the annihilation of Europe's Jews. His mother and younger sister died soon after arriving at Auschwitz, presumably in a gas chamber. Some months later, he and his father were force-marched to another camp—Buchenwald—where the senior Wiesel was beaten to death. By the time Elie Wiesel was freed, on April 10, 1945, he was 16. He did not learn that his two older sisters had survived the camps until months later.

Three days after his camp's liberation, Elie Wiesel saw himself in a mirror, the first time he had seen his reflection in more than a year. "From the depths of the mirror, a corpse gazed back at me. The look in his eyes, as they stared into mine, has never left me."[1] What Wiesel

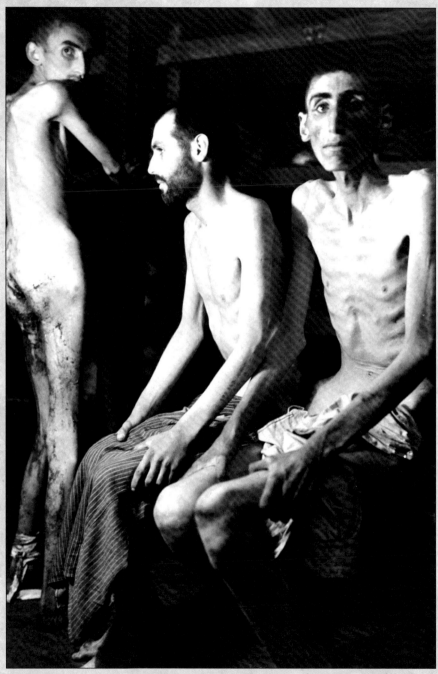

Severely emaciated at the time of their liberation in 1945, these Jews from Russia, Poland, and the Netherlands worked as slave laborers at the Buchenwald concentration camp in Germany—the same camp where author Elie Wiesel was held as a teenager.

lived through, and what continues to haunt his thoughts and dreams, the world now calls the Holocaust—the torture and murder of 6 million Jews by Nazi Germany. In *Night*, Wiesel's landmark memoir, he writes about his first night in Auschwitz:

> Never shall I forget that night, the first night in camp, which has turned my life into one long night, seven times cursed and seven times sealed. Never shall I forget that smoke. Never shall I forget the little faces of the children, whose bodies I saw turned into wreaths of smoke beneath a silent blue sky.
>
> Never shall I forget those flames which consumed my faith forever.
>
> Never shall I forget that nocturnal silence which deprived me, for all eternity, of the desire to live. Never shall I forget those moments which murdered my God and my soul and turned my dreams to dust. Never shall I forget these things, even if I am condemned to live as long as God Himself. Never.[2]

Defining the Holocaust

At least four terms have been used to describe this human tragedy. The Nazis, masters of propaganda, euphemistically called it *Endlösung der Judenfrage*—the "Final Solution of the Jewish Question." In the early 1940s, Eastern European Jews used the Yiddish word *churb'n*, which means "destruction," or the Hebrew term *sho'ah*, which means "catastrophe." The term "holocaust," according to the *Merriam-Webster Online Dictionary*, means "a thorough destruction involving extensive loss of life especially through fire."[3]

Since the end of World War II, the capitalized word "Holocaust" is usually understood to describe what happened to Jews and other groups at the hands of Nazi Germany between 1933 and 1945. According to the United States Holocaust Memorial Museum's website:

The Holocaust was the systematic, bureaucratic, state-sponsored persecution and murder of approximately six million Jews by the Nazi regime and its collaborators. "Holocaust" is a word of Greek origin meaning "sacrifice by fire." The Nazis, who came into power in Germany in 1933, believed that Germans were "racially superior" and that the Jews, deemed "inferior," were an alien threat to the so-called German racial community.[4]

Some scholars insist that the death toll for the Holocaust should include only the 6 million murdered Jews. Others believe the final figures should include all groups targeted by the Nazis for elimination from European society and systematically killed. They believe the numbers should include the mentally or physically disabled; those considered

Major Nazi Camps 1943–1944

NORWAY
Grini — Bredtveit (1942)
Berg (1942)
FINLAND

Vaivara
Klooga
Lagedi

SWEDEN

SOVIET UNION

0   400
Miles

GREAT BRITAIN

IRELAND

Kaiserwald

Horseroed

Front Line January 1944

Bergen-Belsen
Westerbork
Neuengarame
Stutthof Koldichevo
Ravensbrueck
Mechelen
Vught
Sachsenhausen
Treblinka
Breendonk
Dora-Mittelbau
Chelmno
Buchenwald
Gross-Rosen
Trawniki
Compiegne
Fuenfbrunnen
Flossebuerg
Janowska
Drancy
Mauthausen
Starachowice
Vittel
Natzweiler
Plaszow
Struthof
Dachau
Auschwitz
Schirmeck
Gurs
Vorbruck
Bolzano
Rivesaltes
San Sabba
Sajmiste
Fossoli di Carpi
Schabatz

Skarzysko-Karnienna
Majdanek
Sobibor
Budzyn
Belzec
Poniatowa

Caspian Sea

Atlantic Ocean

SPAIN

Nisch

Salonika

Front Line January 1944

REGIONAL BOUNDARIES JANUARY 1944

Mediterranean Sea

Purple squares represent select camps. Because of map scale, not all camps can be shown or labeled. Camps operated by German-allied or dependent states are not shown.

Greater Germany & Occupied Territories

German Allies or Dependent States

Neutrals

Allies

Extermination Camps

Other Camps

racially inferior, such as Gypsies (also known as Romani) and Slavic peoples (Russians, Poles, Latvians, Lithuanians, and others); and those considered threats because of perceived political, ideological, or behavioral differences, such as Communists, Socialists, Jehovah's Witnesses, and homosexuals. If all these groups are included in the death toll of the Holocaust, the total killed increases to as many as 17 million, though the exact number may never be known with certainty.

Hitler's Plan

From 1933 to 1945—the years just before and during World War II—Nazi Germany, under the leadership of Adolf Hitler, instituted a cold-blooded, calculated massacre of all people Hitler felt were inferior. Hitler particularly hated Jews. He blamed them for all of Germany's social and economic problems. He felt Jews were not true Germans and that they were spoiling Germany's racial purity. Eleven years before coming to power, he told a friend, "If I am ever really in power, the destruction of the Jews will be my first and most important job."[5] Hitler's autobiography *Mein Kampf (My Struggle)*, published in two parts—volume 1 in 1925, and volume 2 in 1926—is filled with anti-Jewish writings.

When Hitler was elected chancellor of Germany in 1933, he immediately began to rid the nation of its more than 500,000 Jews. First, the Nazi-controlled government passed laws making it difficult for Jews to make a living or practice their religion. Hitler hoped these restrictive laws would force Jews to leave the country, and many did. Others, however, could not afford to leave, or they could find no country to accept them, forcing them to stay in Germany. Still others, who thought Nazi rule would pass and that life would return to normal, chose to stay.

When Germany invaded Poland in 1939 and the Soviet Union in 1941, Hitler and the Nazis stepped up their anti-Jewish actions. Those Jews who did not die during the invasions were later isolated from non-Jews. All Jews were ordered to move into walled-in neighborhoods called ghettos. Hitler felt it would be easier to begin systematically eliminating them if they were together.

The Nazis' ultimate goal—their "Final Solution to the Jewish Question"—developed over time and was a carefully guarded secret. It involved building prison camps in Germany and Eastern Europe for mass executions. In these concentration camps, people were worked to death, starved, beaten, hanged, shot, gassed, and burned—all in the name of racial purity. Hitler felt that Jews had no right to live in Europe among non-Jews. Under Hitler's "Final Solution," they had no right to live at all.

Chapter 1

What Conditions Led to the Holocaust?

he Holocaust began in 1933, when the Nazi Party and its leader, Adolf Hitler, gained control of the German government. It continued in one form or another until the defeat of Nazi Germany by the armed forces of the Allies—Great Britain, France, the United States, and the Soviet Union, among other nations—and the death of Hitler in 1945. However, the roots of the Holocaust—the bitter resentment and hatred against Jews, known as anti-Semitism—began much earlier. Anti-Semitism had festered in the minds of some European Christians for nearly 2,000 years. Anti-Semitism was an ancient hatred, rising and falling in intensity over the centuries, but it reached its peak in the gas chambers and ovens of Auschwitz, Buchenwald, Bergen-Belsen, and hundreds of other Nazi concentration camps.

Origins of Anti-Semitism in Europe

Prejudice against Jews predates the Christian era. Some Greek and Roman rulers, as early as the third century BC, desecrated Jewish temples and banned their rituals. Written accounts describe violent attacks on Jews, slaughtering thousands. This bias against Jews intensified after the crucifixion of Jesus. Although Jesus was a Jew, his teachings challenged the authority of Jewish leaders, leading them to criticize his message, turn him over to Roman officials for judgment, and call for his crucifixion. Because Jewish leaders incited this act, many Christians harbored a deep-seated hatred, mistrust, and suspicion toward Jews.

Within 1,000 years of Jesus's death the Christian church rose from a humble sect, facing constant persecution and forced to meet in secret, to the most powerful religious, social, and political force in Europe. The Crusades, a series of Christian military campaigns initially meant to seize control of Jerusalem and the Holy Land from Muslim invaders, began in AD 1095. As the Crusades proceeded, other perceived enemies of Christianity, especially Jews, were targeted. During the First and Second Crusades many Jewish communities in Germany were destroyed, and thousands of Jews were massacred. After the Crusades European Jews suffered mass expulsions. All Jews were forcibly expelled from England in 1290, from France in 1396, and from Austria in 1421. Many fled to Poland and Russia where their descendants later suffered at the hands of the Nazi regime.

During the Black Death—epidemics that killed half the population of Europe in the mid-fourteenth century—rumors spread in Europe that Jews had caused the plague by deliberately poisoning water wells. Hundreds of Jewish villages were destroyed as a result of the rumors. Others claimed that Jewish officials kidnapped and murdered Christian children and sacrificed them. For centuries, Jews in Europe were excluded from mainstream society. In many places they were prohibited from certain professions and relegated to those that were considered socially inferior, such as accounting, money lending, and rent collection.

Martin Luther's Anti-Semitism

Anti-Semitism in Germany found a champion in 1543, with the publication of a 60,000-word treatise—*Von den Juden und Ihren Lügen* (*On the Jews and Their Lies*). The author, Martin Luther, was a German priest and theologian who in 1517 had publicly criticized the church in Rome for some of its practices. Luther's criticisms led to a split in the church and to the creation of Protestant denominations. His 1543 treatise, however, dealt exclusively with his feelings of resentment and bitter hatred of Jews in Germany.

After liberating a concentration camp in Germany in April 1945, two US soldiers are greeted by a gruesome sight: a human corpse stuffed inside an oven. Anti-Semitism, already well-established even before the rise of Christianity, reached its peak in Adolf Hitler's Nazi death camps.

In his treatise Luther expressed his opinions about how Jews deserved to be treated. He called Jews "poisonous bitter worms" and wrote that their synagogues (Jewish houses of worship) "should be set on fire, and whatever does not burn up should be covered or spread over with dirt so that no one may ever be able to see a cinder or stone of it." He said Jewish homes should be "broken down or destroyed." He stated that Jews themselves should be "put under one roof, or in a stable, like Gypsies, in order that they may realize that they are not masters in our land." Luther felt Jews should be stripped of their belongings and either put to work at hard labor or driven out of Germany "for all time."[6]

Many scholars point to Luther's treatise as a blueprint for the Holocaust. Ronald Berger, professor of sociology at the University of Wisconsin–Whitewater and author of several books on the Holocaust, credits Luther with "establishing anti-Semitism as a key element of German culture and national identity."[7] Nearly four centuries later, through the rise and fall of the Third Reich (Nazi rule of Germany), few anti-Semitic books or articles were published that failed to quote, or at least mention, Luther's treatise.

Improvement for Some but Not for Others

Attitudes toward Jews by Christians in Western Europe softened considerably in the late 1700s and early 1800s. This was due in part to the ideals of tolerance and equality expressed in documents such as the American Declaration of Independence and Bill of Rights, and the French Declaration of the Rights of Man and of the Citizen. During this period, Jews in Western Europe became active in politics, achieved success in business, medicine, science, and the arts, and were generally accepted in society as equals.

In Eastern Europe, however, conditions remained grim. For centuries in Poland, Jews were afraid to leave their homes during the Easter season, fearing attack by Christians. Some Polish priests urged parishioners to kill Jews to avenge Christ's death. In the Russian Empire at the end of the eighteenth century, empress Catherine the Great decided on a different approach toward her country's Jewish population, which the Nazis later adopted.

In 1792 she decreed that Jews in Russia would be allowed to live only in separate zones called Pales, forbidden to leave them. Within the Pales, Jews had few rights. They could neither own property nor farm, and they were restricted to only a few professions. Most Jews lived in extreme poverty within these ghettos. Throughout Eastern Europe, prejudice against Jews remained volatile. Strict social structures evolved, with Jews invariably at the bottom. According to Martin Gilbert, Oxford University professor of history and Holocaust scholar:

> Church and state both . . . set the Jew aside in the popular mind as an enemy of Christianity and an intruder in the life of the citizen. Jealousies were fermented. Jewish "characteristics" were mocked

and turned into caricatures. The Jew, who sought only to lead a quiet, productive and if possible a reasonably comfortable life, was seen as a leech on society, even when his own struggle to survive was made more difficult by that society's rules and prejudices.[8]

Centuries-old prejudices and a rigid class system denied Eastern European Jews freedoms and privileges that were enjoyed by those in Western Europe during the years approaching World War I.

World War I and the Jews

In the summer of 1914 Archduke Franz Ferdinand of Austria was assassinated by a Serbian national. The assassination, which might have been resolved as a regional issue, quickly escalated into war when Germany supported its ally, the Austro-Hungarian Empire, by declaring war on Russia. Russia had begun to mobilize its troops to support Serbia. Other alliances soon came into play, further widening the conflict. Once the war started, European Jews became involved in the fighting. This time, though, instead of being the target of prejudice and discrimination, they were in uniform, fighting alongside non-Jews for their respective nations in what was called the World War, the Great War, or the War to End All Wars—World War I.

On one side of the conflict were the Central Powers, consisting of the German Empire, the Austro-Hungarian Empire, the Ottoman Empire, and the Kingdom of Bulgaria. Opposing the Central Powers were the Allies, made up of the Triple Entente—the United Kingdom, France, and the Russian Empire—and several smaller nations. The United States joined the war later, on the side of the Allies, to protest the Central Powers' attacks on shipping in international waters. During this truly worldwide conflict, Jews served bravely, facing their country's enemies from the trenches of the Western Front and across the battlefields of Eastern Europe.

More than 100,000 of the 615,000 Jews who lived in Germany at the time served in the German army during World War I. Twelve thousand were killed in action. The first member of the German parliament

On the Jews and Their Lies

In Martin Luther's treatise, *On the Jews and Their Lies*, he refers to Jews not as chosen people of God but as "devil's children." He calls them a "brood of vipers," "useless, evil pernicious people," and "the most vehement enemies of Christ our Lord and of us all." He goes beyond encouraging discrimination and expulsion of Jews from Germany. He condones their murder, thus opening a door to a more drastic solution through which Adolf Hitler and the Nazis, four centuries later, would eagerly march:

> We are at fault in not slaying them [Jews]. Rather we allow them to live freely in our midst despite . . . their murdering, cursing, blaspheming, lying, and defaming; we protect and shield their synagogues, houses, life, and property. In this way we make them lazy and secure and encourage them to fleece us boldly of our money and goods, as well as to mock and deride us, with a view to finally overcoming us, killing us all for such a great sin, and robbing us of all our property (as they daily pray and hope). Now tell me whether they do not have every reason to be the enemies of us . . . to curse us and to strive for our final, complete, and eternal ruin!

Martin Luther, *On the Jews and Their Lies*, Wittenberg, Germany, 1543. www.humanitas-international.org.

to die in action was a Jew—Ludwig Haas. Gilbert explains the participation of European Jews in World War I:

> German Jews fought and died as German patriots, shooting at British Jews who served and fell as British patriots. . . . Man for man, the Jewish and non-Jewish war casualties were in an

almost exact ratio of the respective populations. . . . When the war ended . . . Jewish soldiers, sailors and airmen had filled the Rolls of Honour, the field hospitals and the military cemeteries, side by side with their compatriots under a dozen national flags.[9]

Post–World War I Poland

When World War I officially came to an end on November 11, 1918, the boundaries of many European nations were redrawn. Almost overnight, many of Europe's Jews found themselves living in a different country, without having moved. Three million Jews, living in the German Empire or the Russian Empire at the start of the war, lived in the newly reorganized nation of Poland once the war was over.

In 1919 Poland became one of the founding members of the League of Nations, an international organization designed to prevent future war. The covenant of the league featured a guarantee of the rights of minorities in its member nations, giving Jews in Poland the hope of a peaceful future. Germany eventually joined the league in 1926 but withdrew in 1933 after Hitler rose to power.

The hopes of Jews living in eastern Poland were quickly dashed, however. Two weeks after the signing of the armistice ending the war, Chaim Weizmann, leader of the Zionist Movement in England, wrote to a friend: "Terrible news is reaching us from Poland. The newly liberated Poles there are trying to get rid of the Jews by the old and familiar method which they learnt from the Russians. Heart-rending cries are reaching us."[10] The Zionist Movement advocated the establishment of a Jewish state.

The "terrible news" Weizmann received was accurate. In the final days of World War I, more than 50 Jews were killed by Ukrainians in the eastern Polish city of Lvov. Seventeen hundred more died on February 15, 1919, in Proskurov, Poland, at the hands of a murderous gang that followed Simon Petlura, a Ukrainian nationalist leader. By the end of that year, 60,000 Jews had been killed by Petlura's gangs, victims of local hatred dating back to czarist days.

Humiliation for Germany

With the defeat of the Central Powers in World War I came national humiliation for Germany. The Treaty of Versailles, signed following the war, included punitive measures to prevent Germany from waging war in the future. Large chunks of territory were taken from Germany and put under the control of neighboring nations. Other sections of Germany, such as the Rhineland (the area along either side of the Rhine River, on Germany's western border) were demilitarized and occupied by foreign troops. To make its dishonor worse, Germany's military was reduced to 100,000 troops, with no tanks, no air force, and only a few smaller ships in its navy.

Villagers drop bodies into a mass grave during the epidemic that swept across Europe in the 1300s and came to be known as the Black Death. Europe's Jews were blamed for the deadly plague, leading to the destruction of hundreds of Jewish communities.

Finally, Article 231 of the treaty—known as the "War Guilt Clause"—forced Germany to accept sole responsibility for causing the war and required Germany to pay for all civilian damage caused during the war. The harsh terms of the Versailles Treaty brought shame and economic hardship to the German people. Most Germans felt the terms of the treaty were unfair and humiliating. Revision of the Versailles Treaty became one of the hot topics in Germany during the 1920s, giving rise to several radical right-wing groups, including the Nazi Party.

Beginnings of the Nazi Party

One view among right-wing Germans that reflected the resentment many Germans felt after the war was called *Dolchstosslegende* (the "stab-in-the-back legend"). This view rejected Germany's national responsibility for the war's loss and instead placed it on the shoulders of those members of German society who had failed to rise to the challenge and support the nation's war effort. Groups specifically mentioned were Socialists, Bolsheviks (Communists), and Jews. Political cartoons—such as one showing a stereotypical Jewish man with a raised dagger in his hand, sneaking up behind a German soldier in the trenches of a World War I battlefield—and editorials in German newspapers soon garnered widespread support for this theory.

One group in particular espoused this anti-Semitic attitude. It was a tiny, newly organized right-wing political party officially called the National Socialist German Workers' Party, or *Nationalsozialistische Deutsche Arbeiterpartei* (NSDAP). It became known as the Nazi Party. Its party platform was introduced on February 24, 1920, in a large Munich beer hall. In the speech, one of its authors, speaking to a crowd of about 2,000, outlined the platform's 25 points. Most were nationalistic. At the time, the party had only 60 members.

Point Four of the Nazi platform dealt with how they viewed Jews in Germany: "None but members of the Nation may be citizens of the State. None but those of German blood, whatever their creed, may be members of the Nation. No Jew, therefore, may be a member of the Nation."[11] Another section demanded that all Jews who had come to Germany after 1914 be expelled from the country. The anti-Jewish sections of the platform had been drafted by three members. One, the man who delivered the speech, was a World War I veteran who had been wounded and gassed on the Western Front. His name was Adolf Hitler.

Hitler's Rise

Adolf Hitler was born in Austria on April 20, 1889, the son of a low-ranking customs official. His dream of becoming a great artist led him to Vienna at the age of 19, but he twice failed to gain admission to Vienna's Academy of Fine Arts. Many of the academy's leaders were Jewish. In 1913 he moved to Munich, Germany. Though initially declared unfit for military service, when World War I broke out, Hitler volunteered and was accepted into the German army. He served on the Western Front, achieved the rank of corporal, was wounded in 1916, and gassed two years later. After the war, he returned to Munich amid the chaos of postwar Germany where he eventually joined the Nazi Party and quickly attained leadership.

On August 3, 1921, about a year after his speech in the smoke-filled Munich beer hall outlining his hatred of Jews, Hitler organized the *Sturmabteilung* ("Storm Section") of the party. This group's function was to control the party's membership and harass its opponents. It quickly became known as the SA and its members as Storm Troopers. They proudly marched and demonstrated, wearing brown shirts, gaining them another nickname—Brownshirts. The party's symbol became the swastika, or *Hakenkreuz* ("Hooked Cross"), originally an ancient Sanskrit symbol for fertility used in India. By the time the Storm Troopers were organized, the Nazi Party's membership rolls had risen to 3,000.

The Brownshirts wasted no time making public the anti-Jewish sentiments of the Nazi Party. Gangs of SA members wandered the streets of Munich, attacking individual Jews. They held public street-corner rallies, using crude language to blame Jews for all of Germany's economic woes. In the German city of Nuremberg, a Nazi named Julius Streicher launched a newspaper—*Der Stürmer* (*The Stormer*, or, more

Hyperinflation in Post–World War I Germany

Hyperinflation is a rapid increase in the prices of goods and services, which in turn causes the real value of money to fall. Hyperinflation can lead to financial panic and the collapse of a nation's economy. Most economies try to forestall complete economic collapse by printing additional currency. Robert Edwin Herzstein, author of several books on Nazi Germany, explains how hyperinflation affected Germany in the years after World War I and how this helped lead to the rise of the Nazi Party:

> In April of 1921, the Allied powers finally finished [totaling] their reparations bill and presented it to Germany in the staggering sum of 132 *billion* gold marks. The mark, normally valued at four to the dollar, fell almost instantly to 75. It kept on plummeting—until, by the end of the awful year of 1923, a single U.S. dollar was worth an incredible four billion German marks. German salaries and wages were worthless, purchasing power was nil, the life savings of the middle class had vanished, unemployment passed one million, hundreds of thousands stood in bread lines—and Adolf Hitler tasted opportunity.

Robert Edwin Herzstein and the Editors of Time-Life Books, *The Nazis*. Alexandria, VA: Time-Life Books, 1980, p. 23.

accurately, *The Attacker*)—devoted to portraying Jews as a destructive, evil force. Its initial headline was "The Jews Are Our Misfortune."

In 1923 Hitler tried and failed to seize power in Munich in what came to be called the Munich Beer Hall Putsch (Revolt). For this attempted coup he was sentenced to five years in prison. He served only nine months before being paroled. During his incarceration he composed the first part of an autobiographical work about his life and philosophy. *Mein Kampf (My Struggle)* was published on July 18, 1925. A second volume followed on December 10, 1926. In both, the full venom of Hitler's hatred of Jews became clear.

By 1926 the Nazi Party's membership stood at 17,000, including the black-uniformed SS, the *Schutzstaffeln* ("Protection Squad"), set up a year earlier to provide protection for the Nazi leadership. By 1927 the Nazis were 40,000 strong. In the German national elections in 1928, Nazi candidates secured 12 seats in the country's governing body, the Reichstag.

Economic Depression Brings Added Support for Nazis

An economic depression hit Germany in 1929, part of the worldwide financial crisis known in the United States as the Great Depression. German discontent grew, swelling the ranks of the Nazi Party. In Berlin on January 1, 1930, Storm Troopers attacked and killed eight Jews. During the next nine months, Nazis molested Jews in public places and disrupted synagogue services. In the national election in mid-September 1930, SA thugs terrorized Jewish and Communist voters. To everyone's amazement, when the September 14 election results were tallied, the number of seats in the Reichstag occupied by Nazis rose from 12 to 107. With more than 6 million votes cast in that election for their candidates, the Nazi Party had become the second largest political party in Germany. Nazi political success brought increased harassment of the nation's Jews.

In the presidential election of June 1932, Nazi candidate Adolf Hitler earned more than 36 percent of the votes, coming in second behind the incumbent president, 85-year-old Paul von Hindenburg. By the end of 1932, membership in the Nazi Party exceeded 1.4 million. Hitler and the Nazis had gained enough political backing to demand a coalition government in which Hitler and the Nazi Party would share leadership with Hindenburg. Hindenburg reluctantly agreed and on January 30, 1933, appointed 43-year-old Adolf Hitler chancellor of Germany—the German government's prime minister. Jews in Germany and across Eastern Europe shuddered.

Chapter 2

Prelude to Annihilation

The Holocaust did not begin suddenly in Germany. It evolved over a period of years—from occasional random acts of discrimination and violence to a state-sponsored, all-out effort by Nazi Germany to eliminate those they saw as a threat to their way of life. Michael Berenbaum, project director for the creation of the United States Holocaust Memorial Museum, writes:

> The Holocaust began slowly. Age-old prejudice led to discrimination, discrimination to persecution, persecution to incarceration, and incarceration to annihilation. And mass murder, which culminated with the killing of six million Jews, did not begin with the Jews nor did it encompass only the Jews. The violations of one group's rights are seldom contained only to that group.[12]

German citizens gave in to the Nazis' state-sponsored anti-Semitism for various reasons. Some agreed with Hitler's philosophy—that Jews were a menace to German society and had to be eliminated. Some disagreed but were too meek to speak out, afraid of what others would think of them, or of what might happen to them if they did. Others were indifferent when Jewish colleagues were ousted from their professions. Whatever their motives, according to Sara J. Bloomfield, current director of the United States Holocaust Memorial Museum, German "acceptance emboldened the Nazis to broader and more aggressive action, and, ultimately, their Final Solution."[13] Callous indifference eventually led to the Holocaust. It was *allowed* to happen by everyday Germans.

Hitler Takes Over

Hindenburg and others in the German government hoped Hitler would restore Germany's social order and economic stability without resorting to extreme measures. They were wrong. Almost immediately after being named chancellor, Hitler strengthened his control over the government and its policies. Once in office, his orders bore the legality of the German government.

In February 1933 a suspicious fire broke out in the Reichstag building. Many feared it was a Communist plot to overthrow the government. Some scholars today believe the Nazis set the fire. In any case, Hitler used this event, and its ensuing national panic, to demand emergency powers. Once he had been granted those powers, he moved quickly.

New laws were passed legalizing arbitrary imprisonment without a warrant or trial. These were followed, almost overnight, by mass arrests of the Nazis' political opponents—Socialists, Communists, and Jews. Beginning March 22, 1933, prisoners were taken to the first Nazi prison camp—Dachau, northwest of Munich. There, they were crowded into huts in an abandoned gravel pit, locked behind barbed wire fences. Other camps were soon opened by the SS at Oranienburg, north of Berlin; Esterwegen, near Hamburg; and Lichtenburg, in Saxony. Dachau would later serve as a model for over a thousand concentration camps.

Anti-Jewish Laws Enacted

During the first two months of Nazi rule in Germany, anti-Jewish attacks were largely individual in nature. That changed on April 1, 1933, when Hitler ordered a national boycott of Jewish businesses. Across the country, Nazi Storm Troopers stood outside Jewish shops and at entrances to Jewish law and medical offices to discourage Germans from entering.

Armin Hertz, whose family owned a furniture store in Berlin, remembers:

I saw the Nazi Party members in their brown uniforms and armbands standing in front of our store with signs: "*Kauft nicht bei Juden*" [Don't buy from Jews]. That, of course, was very frightening to us. They marched back and forth all day long. They also put graffiti on the windows of the stores and wrote down "*Jude*" and things like that. Nobody entered the shop. As a matter of fact, there was a competitor across the street—she must have been a member of the Nazi Party already by then—who used to come over and chase people away and say, "Don't buy here, these are Jews."[14]

The message was clear. Jews could leave Germany or suffer the consequences.

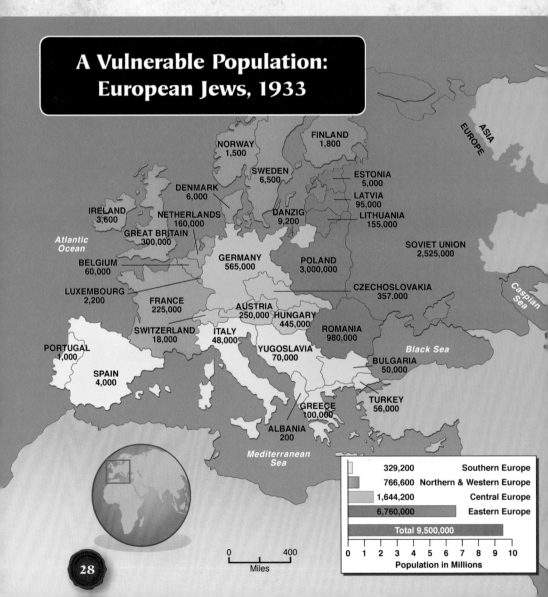

A Vulnerable Population: European Jews, 1933

NORWAY 1,500
FINLAND 1,800
SWEDEN 6,500
DENMARK 6,000
ESTONIA 5,000
LATVIA 95,000
IRELAND 3,600
NETHERLANDS 160,000
DANZIG 9,200
LITHUANIA 155,000
GREAT BRITAIN 300,000
Atlantic Ocean
SOVIET UNION 2,525,000
BELGIUM 60,000
GERMANY 565,000
POLAND 3,000,000
LUXEMBOURG 2,200
CZECHOSLOVAKIA 357,000
FRANCE 225,000
AUSTRIA 250,000
HUNGARY 445,000
ROMANIA 980,000
SWITZERLAND 18,000
ITALY 48,000
YUGOSLAVIA 70,000
Black Sea
PORTUGAL 1,000
BULGARIA 50,000
SPAIN 4,000
TURKEY 56,000
GREECE 100,000
ALBANIA 200
Mediterranean Sea
ASIA
EUROPE
Caspian Sea

	Population	Region
	329,200	Southern Europe
	766,600	Northern & Western Europe
	1,644,200	Central Europe
	6,760,000	Eastern Europe
Total 9,500,000		

0 1 2 3 4 5 6 7 8 9 10
Population in Millions

0 400
Miles

Within a week the Nazis enacted the first of hundreds of national anti-Jewish laws designed to force Jews to leave Germany or, if that failed, to segregate and impoverish them. The first, the April 7 Law for the Restoration of the Professional Civil Service, targeted Jews for removal from governmental service. Paragraph 3, the "Aryan Paragraph," stated that all non-Aryans must retire from their government jobs.

"Aryan" had originally been a linguistic term describing the language of a nomadic group thought to have originated in southeastern Europe and southwestern Asia, and considered by many to be ancestors of Germanic peoples. Under Hitler, Aryan came to mean the opposite of Semitic. To be Aryan, in Hitler's worldview, was the German ideal. To be non-Aryan was to be inferior.

Other anti-Semitic laws followed the April 7 Law almost daily. On April 21 a law passed stating that Jews could no longer obey Jewish law by ritually slaughtering animals to provide themselves kosher meats. On April 25 the Law Against the Overcrowding of German Schools demanded quotas for non-Aryan students in German schools and universities, severely restricting Jewish access to education. Additional laws in April barred Jewish physicians from practicing in hospitals and clinics that were part of the national health insurance system. Pharmacy licenses were no longer available to Jews. Strict limitations on Jewish lawyers came next. By month's end, Jews were banished from German sports organizations. With the Nazis firmly in power, life became increasingly difficult for Jews.

The second half of 1933 brought further restrictions. In July the Nazi Party was declared the only legal political party, and opposition to it was punishable by law. On July 14 another law stripped Jews of Eastern European ancestry of their German citizenship. Also passed on July 14, affecting both Jews and non-Jews, was the Law for the Prevention of Offspring with Hereditary Diseases, which provided for the forced sterilization of parents and potential parents of "defective" children. The Nazis termed such people *Lebensunwertes Leben*—"life unworthy of life." On September 22 German Jews were banned

Book Burning

Nazi Storm Troopers attacked Jewish cultural and intellectual heritage about three months after Hitler became chancellor. On May 10, 1933, book-burnings were held in 30 German university towns by brown-shirted Nazi students and some of their professors. Cast into the flames were thousands of books considered "un-German"—by Jewish and non-Jewish authors alike.

More than 20,000 volumes were consumed in one huge bonfire at *Opernplatz* (Opera House Square), across from the University of Berlin. Enthusiastic crowds eagerly witnessed this spectacle, while listening to speeches proclaiming the death of "Jewish intellectualism." The volumes burned included some written by a German Jewish poet named Heinrich Heine in the 1800s. In his play *Almansor*, Heine had written, "*Dort wo man Bücher verbrennt, verbrennt man am Ende auch Menschen*" ("Where they have burned books, they will end in burning human beings"). Today, his prophetic words are carved into a plaque at the site of the 1933 book-burning.

Quoted in The Quotations Page. www.quotationspage.com.

from art, literature, journalism, music, broadcasting, and theater. By year's end, 30,000 prisoners, Jewish and non-Jewish, occupied Nazi prison camps.

Swearing Allegiance to Hitler

The following year brought additional discriminatory laws. On January 1, 1934, Nazis removed all Jewish holidays from the official German calendar. In April, Germany established its secret state police—the

Gestapo—and the *Volksgericht* (People's Court) to deal with enemies of the state. This court denied the right to a trial by jury and the right to an appeal.

With the death of President Hindenburg in August 1934, Hitler became more than chancellor. Within hours of Hindenburg's death, the positions of chancellor and president were combined, making Hitler the nation's ultimate authority. On the same day, soldiers in the German army were required to swear a personal oath of loyalty to Hitler: "I swear by God this sacred oath: that I shall render unconditional obedience to Adolf Hitler, the *Führer* [leader] of the German Reich, supreme commander of the armed forces, and that I shall at all times be prepared, as a brave soldier, to give my life for this oath."[15] Three weeks later, 90 percent of German voters ratified the change in leadership.

The Nuremberg Laws

In September 1935 Germany passed the Nuremberg Laws, most of which were race laws aimed directly at Jews. Two laws, the Reich Citizenship Law and the Law for the Protection of German Blood and Honor, were centerpieces of this anti-Jewish legislation. The Citizenship Law stated that people of German heritage were citizens with full rights. Those of Jewish heritage were subjects, with no citizenship or civil rights. Without citizenship, Jews could not vote. Without the vote, they were politically powerless. The Law for the Protection of German Blood and Honor was also specifically anti-Jewish. Its provisions claimed the purity of German blood was essential for the nation's success and certain steps were necessary to maintain that purity. One provision prohibited the marriage of a Jew to a non-Jew. Another made extramarital sexual relations between a Jew and a non-Jew a crime.

In addition to laws, race-based curricula were introduced in German schools, offering pseudo-scientific "proof" of the inferiority of Jews, Gypsies, Blacks, Asians, and Arabs. Classroom charts compared Aryan physical characteristics with Jewish ones. For Jewish students, the humiliation was intolerable. One Jewish student who attended school in Breslau, Germany, later remembered the experience. He remembers how it felt as a teenager to be singled out in class:

> [Our teacher] came in and he said, "*Heil Hitler*, students," and we had to stand up and say, "*Heil Hitler*, teacher." Then we had a different curriculum because we had this *Rassenkunde*, which was raceology. That was a regular subject we had. And we were supposed to learn what an Aryan is, the Aryan race. Opposed to the Aryan race, we were the Jews. And the students were to learn what makes the difference between a blond, blue-eyed pure Aryan [and] a Jew. And I hated this biology teacher with a passion. He always pulled me up on my sideburns and he put me in front of the class and you see how, "Here's a Jew," and he started to describe my nose and my cheekbones, and my hair and my features, and how to recognize a Jew. And I was very humiliated. And I hated it.[16]

Children too young to attend school were not spared the anti-Jewish message. A German children's book from 1936 contains the following verse:

> The Devil is the father of the Jew.
> When God created the world,
> He invented the races:
> The Indians, the Negroes, the Chinese,
> And also the wicked creature called the Jew.[17]

Nazis were determined to go to extremes to preserve the purity of Aryan blood. A Jewish doctor, Hans Serelman, gave a life-saving transfusion of his own blood to a non-Jew. For his "crime," he was charged with "race defilement" and sent to a concentration camp for seven months. With so many anti-Jewish laws, it became easy for Nazi officials to accuse Jews of crimes and arrest them. Once arrested, they were sent to prison without a trial. To house them, Hitler ordered the building of additional camps to "concentrate" his opponents and hold them in confined places.

Troubling Years

Between 1934 and 1938, Hitler's Germany rebuilt its armed forces and boldly retook territory that had been taken from it under the terms of the Versailles Treaty at the end of World War I. This included the Rhineland, a strip of land along Germany's western border, on either side of the Rhine River; Austria, to Germany's southeast; and the Sudetenland, a buffer zone between Germany and Czechoslovakia. Although leaders of other nations disapproved, none stood ready to back up their displeasure with force. Once under German control, the civil rights of thousands of Jews in those territories were revoked.

Emboldened by this display of international indifference, Hitler continued to accelerate his anti-Jewish policies within Germany. "Jew-free" villages were encouraged. Signs at the entrances of many cities and towns proclaimed, "Jews Not Wanted Here!" In schools, Jewish

A German elementary school teacher, photographed around 1935, instructs her students in the proper technique for the greeting "Heil, Hitler." This salute and greeting became compulsory under the Nazis; it replaced "good morning" and other similar niceties.

students could not sit on the same bench as non-Jews. On September 7, 1936, the Nazi government imposed a 25 percent tax on all Jewish assets, much higher than taxes imposed on non-Jewish property.

Several more large concentration camps opened in Germany during this period—Sachsenhausen in September 1936, Buchenwald in July 1937, Flossenbürg in May 1938, and Neuengamme in September 1938. Another camp, Mauthausen, was opened in Austria in August 1938. Sachsenhausen was built 15 miles (24.1 km) northeast of Berlin. Its initial purpose was to house political prisoners, but Jews were imprisoned there beginning in 1938.

Nazis sent thousands of political prisoners—Germans who opposed Hitler's actions—to the camps in the years leading up to World War II, including common criminals and Jews. All prisoners received harsh treatment—backbreaking work, insufficient food, unheated housing, and cruel punishment. But Jews were singled out. Nazi officials did not try to hide what happened to prisoners in these early prison camps. They wanted Germans to know, so they would be afraid to speak out against Hitler.

This public harassment of Jews was especially noticeable during the summer of 1938. On June 9, Nazis burned the main synagogue in Munich. They arrested more than 2,000 Jews throughout Germany. On June 15 any Jew previously convicted of a crime—even a traffic violation—was arrested. On July 23 all Jews were ordered to apply for a special identity card that had to be shown to police on demand. On July 25 the licenses of all Jewish doctors were revoked, and on August 10, Nazis destroyed the Great Synagogue in Nuremberg.

No Safe Haven

Each of these events deeply troubled the Jewish community, but Jews had suffered discrimination before. Many hoped such treatment would pass or that they could eventually leave Germany. Leaving the country became less likely beginning July 6, 1938, the start of the Evian Conference at the luxurious French resort, Evian-les-Bain. Representatives

The Witch of Buchenwald

During the eight-year life of the Buchenwald camp, one individual in particular demonstrated the cruelty of German camp officials against those imprisoned there. Ilse Koch, wife of Buchenwald's commandant, Karl Otto Koch, made quite a name for herself for her harsh treatment of prisoners and for her promiscuity with the camp's guards. At her war crimes trial after World War II, witnesses testified that Koch had repeatedly tortured prisoners, sometimes making them commit sexual acts in public. She also accumulated a morbid collection of tattooed skin, taken from the corpses of dead prisoners.

Koch, who had been born in 1906, began her service to the Reich in 1936 at the Sachsenhausen concentration camp near Berlin. She and her husband later moved to Buchenwald, where he served as camp commandant until being transferred to Majdanek, another concentration camp just outside Lublin, Poland. Though her sadistic practices continued wherever she went, it was the prisoners of Buchenwald who gave her the name *Die Hexe von Buchenwald*, "The Witch of Buchenwald." She committed suicide in a German prison in 1967.

of 32 nations attended the conference at the request of American president Franklin D. Roosevelt. Roosevelt had hoped the nations would agree on a way to provide safe haven for Europe's Jews. Despite his hopes, one by one the nations of the world expressed their sympathy for the Jewish situation but made excuses for not accepting massive numbers of Jewish refugees.

With foreign shores no longer available for most of Germany's Jews, the Nazis had to find another solution to their "Jewish problem."

The first hint of that solution occurred in November 1938. It came to be called *Kristallnacht*—Night of Broken Glass.

Kristallnacht

In late October Nazi officials decided to deport Jews who had originally possessed Polish citizenship back to Poland. They rounded them up, forced them to abandon most of their possessions, crammed them into railroad cars, transported them to the border, and marched them into Poland. The Polish government did not want to readmit them, so the Jews were herded into makeshift concentration camps near the Polish town of Zbaszyn. Housed in old stables still full of horse dung and given little food, their situation soon became dire.

One Polish Jew, Zindel Grynszpan, managed to send a postcard to his 17-year-old son Herschel, who was in school in Paris, telling him about their plight. Herschel Grynszpan received his father's correspondence on November 7, 1938. Enraged by the news of his family's treatment, he went to the German embassy and killed a young Nazi diplomat named Ernst vom Rath. When news of the death of a Nazi official by a Polish-German Jew reached Germany, the response was immediate.

On November 9, Nazi propaganda minister Joseph Goebbels, with Hitler's approval, ordered a nationwide pogrom against Jews. A pogrom is a mob attack or riot that has been approved or condoned by a ruling government and that is directed against a particular group of people. Pogroms are characterized by widespread killings and the destruction of homes, businesses, and places of worship.

Nazi officials later claimed that the ensuing riots and destruction that took place over the next 24 hours were the result of public outrage—spontaneous citizen-led actions. However, at 11:55 p.m., November 9, Gestapo chief Heinrich Müller sent telegrams to all police stations in Germany and German-occupied Austria, informing his subordinates that he did not want them interfering with actions that targeted Jews, their businesses, their synagogues, or their homes.

According to the authors of *The Holocaust Chronicle*, the attacks that night against Germany's Jews "were devastating":

> Throughout the Reich, Jewish synagogues, cemeteries, hospitals, schools, businesses, and homes were looted, wrecked and often set aflame. Scores of Jews were killed; thousands more were arrested and marched off to concentration camps. The Jews' German neighbors inflicted much of this damage, while police not only followed Müller's orders not to interfere but went on to arrest many of those who had been victimized. Meanwhile, fire brigades followed their orders, too: Let torched synagogues burn, but protect Aryan property nearby. *Kristallnacht* ended the illusion that anything resembling normal Jewish life was still possible in the Third Reich.[18]

Arthur Flehinger, a Jew from Baden-Baden, Germany, witnessed the actions of one mob. On November 10, a group of 60 Jewish men were ordered to assemble in the street and were marched to the local synagogue. Inside, they were met by zealous Nazi officers and SS men. Flehinger was ordered to the podium where normally passages of the Torah, the first five books of the Bible—the Books of Moses—would be read. There, at the insistence of his Nazi captors, he read aloud to his fellow Jews a particularly anti-Semitic passage from Adolf Hitler's book *Mein Kampf*. According to Flehinger:

> I read the passage quietly, indeed so quietly that the SS man posted behind me repeatedly hit me in the neck. Those who had to read other passages after me were treated in the same manner. After these "readings" there was a pause. Those Jews who wanted to relieve themselves were forced to do so against the synagogue walls, not in the toilets, and they were physically abused while doing so.[19]

Following this humiliation, the Jews were led outside and forced to watch helplessly as their synagogue was set on fire. Flehinger states that one SS man told him, "'If it had been my decision, you would have perished in that fire.'"[20]

On that same morning—November 10, 1938—the streets of most German and Austrian cities were littered with the broken glass of thousands of smashed Jewish storefront windows. More than 7,000 Jewish shops and over 1,000 synagogues were damaged, looted, or destroyed during the 24-hour *Kristallnacht*. Thirty thousand Jewish men were sent to concentration camps. Most were later released, but only if they could prove they were about to emigrate and would transfer their property to the Nazi government before leaving the country. Nearly 1,000 died in the camps. In the weeks following the pogrom, Nazi officials decided that the damage incurred to the national economy as a result of the destruction was the fault of Jews and would have to be paid by the Jewish community.

Fear and Suspicion

From *Kristallnacht* onward, life for Jews in the Third Reich became more and more difficult to bear. Neighbors were openly hostile, Jews were forced to wear yellow stars marked *Jude* on their clothes, and they were prevented from making more than the most meager of livings to support themselves. In the months leading to Germany's invasion of Poland in September 1939, Jews in Germany and occupied territories were watched more closely. Josef Stone, a Jew who grew up in Frankfurt, Germany, remembers:

> We never felt comfortable. At least I didn't. . . . You didn't trust your next-door neighbor because you didn't know what they were going to do to you. Neighbors who formerly came to your house, and were neighborly and friendly, all of a sudden refrained from even saying hello to you. They acted as if they didn't know you. I can't say that they were really trying to do something to you, but they were afraid that if they would show you any kind of friendliness that they would have a problem.[21]

Another German Jew, Hermann Gottfried, originally from Berlin, recalls, "You just had to be careful in everything you did. Being a Jew, you were marked. The common people, they were watching you. They were all detectives in civilian clothes, like the FBI in a corner watching you."[22] The invasion of Poland by Germany on September 1, 1939, brought Poland under Nazi control. Jews were herded together, starved, overworked, tortured, and murdered. The fate of Eastern Europe's Jews was sealed.

Chapter 3

The Road to Auschwitz

Early in 1939 German Jews were still free to leave Germany, but thanks in part to the results of the Evian Conference and German laws that stripped them of most of their wealth, they had few places to go and little money with which to pay their passage. Doors that had been closed to Jews remained closed, and doors that had once been open began closing. In Palestine on May 17, Jewish immigration was severely limited by the British government, which ruled the region. In the United States, quotas continued to restrict immigration, and a 1939 Gallup poll showed 83 percent of Americans opposed the admission of large numbers of Jewish refugees.

In Germany, too, official policy became harsher, as did Hitler's view of the future. On January 30, 1939, Hitler delivered a speech to the Reichstag about the future of Germany and the fate of Europe's Jews. His words, mostly a tirade against what he perceived as Jewish-influenced Western governments threatening war if he continued Germany's expansion, were ominous:

> In the course of my life I have very often been a prophet, and have usually been ridiculed for it. . . . Today I will once more be a prophet: if the international Jewish financiers in and outside Europe should succeed in plunging the nations once more into a world war, then the result will not be the Bolshevising [making Communist] of the earth, and thus a victory of Jewry, but the annihilation of the Jewish race in Europe![23]

In this speech, Hitler did not detail what steps he had in mind to accomplish that end. However, over the next six years he referred to his "prophecy" about the fate of the Jewish people in Europe at least a dozen times, each time making his wishes clear to his underlings. Before those wishes could be fulfilled, though, Hitler felt Germany needed room—what he called *Lebensraum* (living space).

Invasion Leads to War

On March 15, 1939, Nazi troops entered Czechoslovakia. No nation acted to prevent the invasion, so Czechoslovakia, like the Rhineland, Austria, and the Sudetenland before it, disappeared from the map, becoming *Lebensraum* for the Third Reich. Once again, Jews in newly occupied territories lost their civil rights and became trapped. On the morning of September 1, 1939, Nazi forces crossed into Poland. Two days after the invasion, Britain and France declared war on Germany, officially beginning World War II.

During Germany's invasion of Poland, Jews fought alongside non-Jews in the Polish army, trying desperately to protect their country from the invading Nazi army. Thousands of Jews died in aerial bombardments of western Polish cities, while others died at the hands of Nazi soldiers. Most were killed by *Einsatzgruppen*, special SS killing squads ordered to carry out Operation Tannenberg, singling out Jews for "special treatment." In one Polish village on September 3, an SS group seized 20 prominent Jews, marched them to the marketplace, and executed them in view of their families. In another village, the few survivors of a Nazi bombardment were told to run. When they did, *Einsatzgruppen* commandos shot them down.

According to Martin Gilbert, such actions were commonplace in the first days of the invasion:

In the first ten days of the German advance . . . onslaughts against unarmed, defenceless civilians were carried out in more than a hundred towns and villages. In the city of Czestochowa, home of thirty thousand Jews, 180 Jews were shot on September

4, "Bloody Monday." At the village of Widawa, home of one hundred Jewish families, the Germans ordered the rabbi, Abraham Mordechai Morocco, to burn the Holy Books. He refused, whereupon they burned him, with the Scrolls of the Law in his hands. On September 8, in the city of Bedzin, where more than twenty thousand Jews lived, two hundred were driven into the synagogue, which was then locked and set on fire.[24]

Within a month of the invasion Poland surrendered, leaving its 3.3 million Jews at the mercy of the Nazis. In the first two months of German occupation, 5,000 Jews were murdered by SS troops behind the lines as Nazi forces advanced across western Poland.

The Polish Jewish Problem

The issue of Jews in western Poland was different for the Nazis than it had been in Germany. For one thing, by September 1939 only a few hundred thousand Jews were left in Germany—less than 1 percent of the country's total population. In contrast, 393,950 Jews lived in Warsaw, Poland's capital, more than in all of Germany. In 1939 Jews made up one-third of Warsaw's population and 10 percent of the entire population of Poland.

One Nazi who thought he knew how to handle the problem was Adolf Eichmann, head of the Office of Jewish Emigration and considered the Third Reich's "Jewish specialist." He proposed the Nisko Plan, which would resettle all Jews onto a huge reservation—the Lublin-Lipowa Reservation—in the least hospitable part of the Nazi empire. This was the administrative area called *Generalgouvernement*, or General Government, that had been created in central Poland by Berlin on October 10, 1939.

Eichmann's plan was approved, and the first trainload of Jews arrived on October 18, 1939. According to Laurence Rees, author of numerous books on the Holocaust:

Conditions [in the General Government] were appalling. Little or no preparation was made for the Jews' arrival, and many

Rudoph Höss's Dachau Training

On April 30, 1940, SS *Hauptsturmführer* (Captain) Rudolf Höss was appointed commandant of Auschwitz. Six years earlier, he had begun his career as a concentration camp guard at Dachau. Author Laurence Rees explains Dachau's influence on Höss after his arrival there in November 1934:

> The next three and a half years at Dachau were to play a defining role in shaping Höss' character: For the carefully conceived regime at Dachau—inspired by Theodor Eicke, the first commandant of the camp—was not just brutal; it was designed to break the will of the inmate. Eicke channeled the violence and hatred that the Nazis felt toward their enemies into systems and order. Dachau is infamous for the physical sadism practiced there: Whippings and other beatings were commonplace. Prisoners could be murdered and their deaths dismissed as "killed whilst attempting escape"—and a significant minority of those sent to Dachau did die there. The real power of the regime at Dachau, however, lay less in physical abuse—terrible as it undoubtedly was—and more in mental torture.

Laurence Rees, *Auschwitz: A New History*. New York: PublicAffairs, 2005, p. 6

died. This was a matter of no concern to the Nazis—indeed it was something to be encouraged. As Hans Frank, one of the most senior Nazis at work in Poland, put it when addressing his staff in November 1939: "Don't waste time on the Jews. It is a joy to finally be able to deal with the Jewish race. The more that die the better."[25]

By January 30, 1940, an estimated 78,000 Jews from Germany, Austria, and Czechoslovakia had been deported to the Lublin-Lipowa Reservation.

Eichmann's Nisko Plan ultimately failed, due to the logistical nightmare of trying to relocate three separate masses of people—Jews and non-Jewish Poles being moved out, and Germans being moved in to resettle the region once all the "undesirables" had been moved out—all at the same time. However, another plan—one that created ghettos in some of Poland's largest cities—was implemented, having disastrous results for Poland's Jews.

Ghettos

On September 21, 1939, Reinhard Heydrich, head of Germany's Central Security Office, sent a message to *Einsatzgruppen* commanders in Poland. Jews were to be put into ghettos—isolated, walled-off areas—in large cities like Warsaw and Lodz. The term "ghetto" was first used in Venice, Italy, in 1516, to refer to a section of the city occupied only by Jews. To the Nazis, ghettos were temporary concentration camps—holding pens for those they wanted to eliminate from Third Reich society.

Jews were to be gathered together in cities for three reasons. Nazis wanted to rid large areas of the Polish countryside of Jews—to make them *Judenrein*, "cleansed of Jews." This, Heydrich said, would make room for German settlement. Secondly, Jews could be used as a handy labor force to manufacture items needed for the Nazi war effort. Finally, the Nazis wanted Jews kept near major railways, where it would be easier to ship them to concentration camps, or, as Heydrich phrased it, to facilitate "a better possibility of control and later deportation."[26]

Ghettoization began on October 8 with the creation of a ghetto in Piotrków Trybunalski, Poland. On October 19 a second ghetto was established at Lublin. All Jews who lived outside the ghettos were ordered to move within their confines, forced to abandon homes, livelihoods,

LAND

DENMARK

SWEDEN

North
Sea

NETHERLANDS

GREAT
BRITAIN

BELGIUM

Riga

Liepaja

Baltic
Sea

Siauliai

Kovno

Vilna

Dvinsk

OCCUPIED
EASTERN
TERRITORY

Mogilev

Grodno

Lida

Minsk

Bialystok

Brest-
Litovsk

Lachva

Gomel

Warsaw

Lublin

Pinsk

Lodz

Kielce

Kovel

Rovno

Czestochowa

Theresienstadt

Krakow

Tarnow

Lvov

Vinnitsa

PROTECTORATE
OF BOHEMIA
AND MORAVIA

Stry

Chortkov

GREATER GERMANY

SLOVAKIA

Kolomyia

Mogilev-Podolsk

Kosice

Chernovtsy

Kherson

FRANCE

Miskolc

Uzhgorod

Dej

Kishinev

Budapest

HUNGARY

Odessa

SWITZERLAND

Szeged

Kaposvar

Cluj

Tirgu-
Mures

Atlantic
Ocean

ITALY

CROATIA

ROMANIA

Black
Sea

SERBIA

SPAIN

Corsica

BULGARIA

Salonika

ALBANIA

Sardinia

Front Line
January 1944

GREECE

TURKEY

Mediterranean
Sea

1944 INTERNATIONAL BOUNDARIES

Ghettos Established
1939–May 1941

German-Occupied

Ghettos Established
June 1941–1943

German Ally

Neutral

Ghettos Established
1944

Liberated/Allies

0   300

Miles

Ghettos in Occupied Europe 1939–1944

and possessions. Early in 1940 another ghetto was established in a largely neglected region of Lodz. Of the 31,721 apartments there—most of which had but one room—only 725 had running water. Into that ghetto, 160,000 Jews were moved. On May 1, 1940, the Lodz ghetto's gates were sealed.

One building in the Auschwitz concentration camp—Block 11—did much to maintain discipline. It also reflected the brutality of those in charge of the camp. From the outside, Block 11 looked much like the other red-brick barracklike buildings in the camp. However, its purpose, which was quickly known to all in the camp, struck fear into the hearts of inmates. Block 11 was a torture chamber.

Jerzy Bielecki was a Polish prisoner at Auschwitz who saw inside Block 11 and survived to tell about it. He had hidden himself to avoid a work detail and had been caught and sent there for punishment. When he entered the building's attic, he heard moaning and smelled a foul stench. He saw a man hanging from a beam by his hands, which had been tied behind his back. "The SS man brought a stool and said, 'Climb on it,'" he later wrote. "I put my hands behind my back and he took a chain and tied them." Without warning, the guard kicked the stool from underneath him. The pain was excruciating. After an hour, he said, "my shoulders were breaking out from their joints." Bielecki was crippled by his ordeal.

Quoted in Laurence Rees, *Auschwitz: A New History*. New York: PublicAffairs, 2005, p. 26.

The Warsaw Ghetto

In October 1940 Ludwig Fischer, the German governor of Warsaw, announced that all Jews living outside the predominantly Jewish district of Warsaw had to move into that district. Whatever belongings they could bring by hand or cart were allowed. All other possessions had to be left behind. Once the ghetto was established, Jews, one-third of Warsaw's population, were to occupy less than 2.5 percent of the city's area. With only 27,000 apartments in the ghetto, six or seven people were forced to share each room. Nine-foot-tall brick walls (2.7 m) were erected by Jewish laborers to encircle the ghetto. Those walls were sealed on November 15, 1940, cutting off Warsaw's 400,000 Jews from the outside world.

Conditions were harsh in the ghettos. In the Warsaw ghetto, for example, a half-million Jews were crowded into an area of only 3.5 square miles (9.1 sq km). Starvation, cold temperatures, contagious diseases, and overwork in forced labor gangs killed tens of thousands over time. Ten percent of the Warsaw ghetto's population—40,000 individuals—died the first year. One Polish survivor remembers:

> People were pushed in like sardines. And they kept on bringing more and more people every single day, and there was no room anymore to put them in. The windows were boarded up. We were not allowed to look out the window, ever. Everything was boarded up. We were not allowed to go out and get water. Every day there were different decrees. "Jews turn in your bicycles. Jews turn in your valuables. Jews turn in your winter coats. [Jewish] children are not allowed to go to school. Jews, don't walk on sidewalks." Of course, we had to walk on the streets, and the Germans had the pleasure of riding over us with cars, with anything they wanted to hit us.[27]

Nazi cruelty in the ghettos was commonplace. Thousands of Holocaust survivors have recalled witnessing atrocities. Some occurred because of a violation of one of the hundreds of rules enforced upon ghetto residents. Others happened because of Jewish resistance to Nazi rule. Still others resulted from Nazi soldiers who simply enjoyed humiliating Jews for entertainment. One survivor of both the Warsaw and Lodz ghettos, Mary Berg, wrote in her diary on November 2, 1939, what she saw from her window:

> A man with markedly Semitic [Jewish] features was standing quietly on the sidewalk near the curb. A uniformed German

approached him and apparently gave him an unreasonable order, for I could see that the poor fellow tried to explain something with an embarrassed expression. Then a few other uniformed Germans came upon the scene and began to beat their victim with rubber truncheons. They called a cab and tried to push him into it, but he resisted vigorously. The Germans then tied his legs together with a rope, attached the end of the rope to the cab from behind, and ordered the driver to start. The unfortunate man's face struck the sharp stones of the pavement, dyeing them red with blood. Then the cab vanished down the street.[28]

Berg also reported that Nazi soldiers sometimes gathered Jewish couples into a room, made them strip naked, and forced them to dance together to the accompaniment of a playing phonograph, all to entertain the soldiers. Another ghetto survivor reports, "I saw with my own eyes Germans tossing [Jewish] babies in the air and shooting them. I couldn't believe it, but I saw it. It did happen! And they were laughing as they were doing this."[29]

At roughly the same time the ghettos were opened, another program was being implemented in Germany to eliminate other undesirables. This program, begun on a small scale, would eventually lead to the establishment of Nazi camps specifically designed for killing.

Hitler's Euthanasia Projects

In early 1939 the Nazi government established the Reich Committee for Scientific Research of Hereditary and Severe Constitutional Diseases. Its purpose was to identify and put to death deformed or retarded children. Doctors and nurses, midwives, and hospital administrators identified the children, who were then sent to special children's centers in one of 21 hospitals, where most were killed by lethal injection. Thus, Nazis eliminated those children they considered a burden. A similar though more extensive program aimed at deformed or retarded adults came later that year.

Frightened Jews, including many women and children, surrender to Nazi soldiers in Poland's Warsaw ghetto in 1943. Ghetto residents were subjected to cold, starvation, and brutality—their plight made worse by their isolation from the outside world.

In October 1939 Hitler signed a memo authorizing certain German doctors to kill adult patients whom some German scientists had deemed "useless eaters."[30] In the memo, Hitler said he was issuing the order "so that patients who, on the basis of human judgment, are considered incurable, can be granted a mercy death after a discerning diagnosis."[31] This order led to the euthanasia of mentally and physically handicapped German and Austrian citizens whom the Nazis considered unworthy to represent the Third Reich and whom they deemed an economic burden on the state. The order was predated to September 1, 1939—to the start of the war—to give the impression that its actions were a wartime necessity.

The Nazis wanted to devise a killing system that would not overly alarm the patient beforehand and that could be easily concealed from the public. Carbon monoxide gas poisoning was used most often, but Hitler's personal physician, Karl Brandt, reported to him that a rat poison known by the brand name Zyklon B, which released cyanide gas, had also been successful. Zyklon B eventually became the poison gas of choice in some Nazi death camps.

Medical personnel chose patients to be euthanized from lists provided by hospitals, nursing homes, and other public health facilities. Patients selected were transported to one of six euthanasia centers in Germany and Austria—Hartheim, Sonnenstein, Grafneck, Hadamar, Brandenburg, and Bernburg. Doctors and nurses at these facilities used two methods at first—starvation and lethal injection—to kill their patients, but eventually, the favorite method became gassing with carbon monoxide in chambers disguised as tiled showers. Once the patients had been killed, gold teeth were harvested from corpses before they were burned in crematoria. Families of those killed were notified that their loved one had died of a heart attack or pneumonia, and that the body had been cremated for public health reasons.

The Nazis called their euthanasia project Operation T-4. It was responsible for the deaths of 70,000 to 80,000 people, including 4,000 to 5,000 Jews. Techniques developed for T-4 were later incorporated into special concentration camps designed for mass extermination.

The Camps

According to the United States Holocaust Memorial Museum's website, the term "concentration camp"—*Konzentrationslager* in German—is "a camp in which people are detained or confined, usually under harsh conditions and without regard to legal norms of arrest and imprisonment that are acceptable in a constitutional democracy."[32] The term was first used to describe camps built by the British in South Africa to contain Boer prisoners during the Second Anglo-Boer War, which lasted from 1899 to 1902.

The first concentration camps in Nazi Germany were established just after Hitler was appointed chancellor in 1933. They originally housed political opponents but later were used to detain criminals and others thought to be threats to the state. In 1934 Hitler authorized the leader of the SS, Heinrich Himmler, to create a centralized administration of the camps, formalizing them into a centrally controlled system. Himmler chose former Dachau commandant Theodor Eicke as the system's head. Other authorities could build forced-labor camps and detention camps, but after December 1934 the SS became the only agency in the Reich authorized to establish and manage facilities that were formally called concentration camps.

As Germany expanded its borders in 1938 and 1939, the numbers of those considered enemies of the state increased, requiring additional camps. By the time Nazi forces invaded Poland in September 1939, six large concentration camps were within the Reich: Dachau, founded in 1933; Sachsenhausen, in 1936; Buchenwald, in 1937; Flossenbürg (built in northeastern Bavaria), in 1938; Mauthausen (near Linz, Austria), also in 1938; and Ravensbrück, the women's camp (southeast of Berlin), in 1939.

Persons imprisoned in these camps were forced to do hard physical labor, in most cases as construction workers, building the camp structures in which they were to live. By 1938 Himmler and other SS leaders began using the large workforce on projects for the Reich, such as quarrying stone, making brick, mining coal, and excavating. Locations for new camps were determined based upon their proximity to mines, quarries, and other sites important to the German economy. Backbreaking work with only slim rations killed many prisoners, but once World War II began, the camps were increasingly used as sites where SS authorities could kill targeted groups. Working people to death was just one form of killing them. Many Jews meekly accepted their fate, but others, despite overwhelming odds, resisted.

Resistance

Jewish resistance to Nazi cruelty took many forms. It ranged from small, secret acts of defiance to open armed rebellion. When anti-Jewish laws first ordered their businesses and synagogues closed, many Jews ignored the law. They conducted business in secret and worshipped in

Nazi Germany "Euthanasia" Centers, 1940–1945

GREATER GERMANY

Vistula

Bug

SOVIET UNION

Ruhr

Weser

Bernburg

Brandenburg

Elbe

Oder

GENERAL GOUVERNEMENT

Rhine

Hadamar

Main

Sonnenstein

PROTECTORATE OF BOHEMIA AND MORAVIA

FRANCE

Grafeneck

Inn

Danube

March

SLOVAKIA

0   150
Miles

Hartheim

SWITZERLAND

Drava

HUNGARY

Euthanasia Methods
■ Gas
■ Lethal Injections

ITALY

1939 REGIONAL BOUNDARIES

their homes. When Jewish children could no longer attend school, their parents taught them at home. When Nazis began arresting Jews and sending them to concentration camps, many others went into hiding. A few managed to stay hidden for the duration of the war.

Some German Jews defied Hitler's plan by leaving the country. Others knew that older members of their families could not make the trip, so they stayed behind to care for them. Still others, sensing the dangers to come, left their homes and joined organized bands of fighters in remote forests. These resistance groups armed themselves and sabotaged Nazi efforts, blowing up bridges and railroad tracks, cutting telephone wires, and ambushing troops. In ghettos and concentration camps, many Jews defied orders by smuggling food, holding religious ceremonies in secret, attempting escape, and even blowing up buildings and killing guards.

The most famous ghetto revolt occurred in the Warsaw ghetto on January 18, 1943, when Jews rebelled against a deportation order that would have sent 8,000 of them to concentration camps. Jews went into hiding, refusing to show up for deportation. Resistance fighters, armed with iron rods, Molotov cocktails, and a few pistols and hand grenades that had been smuggled into the ghetto, attacked German forces, driving them from the ghetto. Nazi troops returned in force, however, on April 19, 1943, storming the ghetto and burning its buildings one by one. Despite being vastly outnumbered, the 700–750 resistance fighters managed to hold off Nazi infantry and tanks until mid-May. When news of the revolt leaked out, it inspired Jewish resistance elsewhere.

Most Jews during the war knew they could not free themselves from Nazi control. They had few weapons, no powerful allies, and nowhere to run. All they could do was fight for their own dignity. Survival became the ultimate resistance. Survivors wanted to live long enough to tell others what the Nazis had done, especially what they had done in their most infamous camp—Auschwitz.

Auschwitz

After the invasion of Poland, Germany needed still more camps to hold political prisoners, resistance fighters, and those considered racially inferior—like Jews and Gypsies. Among the new camps were Gusen, built in 1939; Neuengamme, built near a major brickworks in 1940; and Gross-Rosen, Auschwitz, and Natzweiler, all built in 1940. Of those camps, Auschwitz has come to represent the worst of the Holocaust.

The story of Auschwitz began on April 27, 1940, when Himmler decided that a new camp needed to be built on the site of a former Polish army barracks near Oświecim, Poland. *Oświecim* in German is *Auschwitz*. The first prisoners arrived at the newly constructed camp in June 1940, but they were neither Polish nor Jewish. They were 30 German criminals, transferred from Sachsenhausen. They became the camp's first Kapos, inmates who served as the Nazis' assistants within the camp. They enforced order, helped select prisoners for work details, and turned prisoners in for punishment in exchange for better food, better clothing, or other special favors. Many Kapos were particularly cruel, but the culture of brutality in Nazi concentration camps was created by each camp's SS guards.

One Holocaust scholar explains Auschwitz's significance:

> The camp's original mission was to be a regional prison for Poles who opposed German rule. That purpose made Auschwitz a deadly place for tens of thousands of non-Jewish Poles who were killed by slave labor, disease, and execution. In the months and years ahead, Auschwitz would expand into a network of labor and killing installations that would destroy more than a million people. Ninety percent were Jews. They came not only from Poland but from every part of Nazi-controlled Europe. Eventually, Auschwitz revealed . . . Nazi racism to such an extent that Auschwitz became nearly synonymous with the Holocaust itself.[33]

Auschwitz was originally intended as a "quarantine" camp to hold prisoners awaiting transport to other camps, but under the command of Rudolf Höss it became apparent that it would serve as a place of permanent imprisonment. Rees writes: "No one on that first day—and that certainly included Rudolf Höss—could have predicted the camp would, within five years, become the site of the largest mass murder the world has yet seen."[34]

Chapter 4

Mass Murder

Mid-1941 was a turning point in Nazi Germany's policy toward Jews. Events that took place that summer doomed Europe's Jews—those in occupied countries of Western Europe, those already interned in Nazi concentration camps, those crowded into the ghettos of western Poland, and those living in the western Soviet Union.

The Nazi invasion of the Soviet Union, which began on June 22, was one of these events. During this invasion, as they had in the 1939 invasion of Poland, *Einsatzgruppen* followed combat troops into conquered territory to eliminate enemies of the Reich. Another event that helped accelerate the pace of killing by the Third Reich was a severe food shortage predicted to happen in the Lodz ghetto in July 1941. This expected shortage led to a change in the Nazis' attitude toward the usefulness of Jewish ghettos and eventually to a change in official policy toward Jews.

By June 22, 1941, the number of Jews killed by Nazi Germany had approached 100,000. During the following year, that number increased tenfold. The events of the summer of 1941 resulted in the formulation of official German state policy for the annihilation of millions over the next four years.

Operation Barbarossa

On June 22, 1941, the German High Command launched Operation Barbarossa, the invasion of the Soviet Union. Nazi troops crossed through Soviet-occupied eastern Poland and then into the Soviet Union itself. Nazi troops advanced toward Moscow, the Soviet capital, and into Soviet-controlled Lithuania, Latvia, and Estonia. Behind them came *Einsatzkommandos*, soldiers specially trained to hunt down and execute nonmilitary enemies of the Reich. Four units crisscrossed Ukraine, Belorussia, Latvia, and Lithuania. Group commanders at first recruited local anti-Semites to eliminate the local Jewish population. Nazis referred to these operations as "self-cleansing."

When Operation Barbarossa began, Nazi policy toward the murder of Soviet Jews seems not to have been clear-cut. All of Hitler's underlings knew how he felt about Jews in general. Each remembered the Führer's 1939 Reichstag speech in which he predicted the "extermination" of European Jews if they "caused" a world war, but he never issued any orders specifically dealing with this issue. During the summer of 1941, however, official state policy toward Jews changed.

A Step Toward the Final Solution

In mid-July 1941 a report reached Adolf Eichmann's office about conditions in Polish ghettos. A severe food shortage was expected at Lodz, and Rolf-Heinz Höppner, head of the Security Service in the region, suggested a possible solution to "the Jewish problem": "There is the danger this winter that the Jews can no longer all be fed. It is to be seriously considered whether the most humane solution might not be to finish off those Jews not capable of working by some sort of fast-working preparation. This would be in any event more pleasant than letting them starve."[35] Höppner's report must have caused a change in thinking in the upper echelon of Nazi leadership; weeks later, orders came from Berlin to *Einsatzgruppen* commanders that led to a significant increase in killing Jewish civilians.

On July 31, just over a month after Operation Barbarossa began, Hermann Göring, second only to Hitler in the Third Reich, sent a message to Reinhard Heydrich, authorizing him to prepare for what, by that time, had come to be officially called "The Final Solution of the Jewish Problem." Heydrich's plan led to a conference in early 1942, where specific steps were outlined for the construction of death camps with gas chambers, designed for the mass murder of every Jew under Nazi control. Before those camps were finished, however, the Nazis had to use more traditional means to kill.

A member of the Einsatzgruppen, *a unit of soldiers specially trained to hunt down and execute nonmilitary enemies of the Third Reich, prepares to shoot a Polish Jew who kneels at the edge of a mass grave already filled with many bodies.*

The Massacres at Uman and Babi Yar

In September 1941 *Einsatzkommandos* stepped up their actions. During the months following the invasion, according to the authors of *The Holocaust Chronicle*:

> . . . these mobile killing units devastated hundreds of Jewish communities, slaughtering more Jews than the Nazis had murdered in the previous eight years. About 1.3 million Jews (about a quarter of all the Jews who died in the Holocaust) were killed, one by one, by the 3,000 men in the four *Einsatzgruppen*, their support troops, local police, and collaborators—all with the assistance of the *Wehrmacht* [armed forces]. Most of the 1.3 million murders occurred in 1941.[36]

The most notorious mass murder committed by *Einsatzgruppen* began in Uman, Ukraine, and ended two weeks later at Babi Yar, a ravine-filled area in northwestern Kiev, one of Ukraine's largest cities. On September 16, 1941, Nazi officials ordered Jews to report to the Uman airport for a census. Those who reported were marched to an area where long ditches had been excavated. Tables were set up for the "census," but soon units of *Einsatzkommandos* took positions around the area. Once they were in place, the killing began.

A regular German army officer, Erwin Bingel, witnessed the event and later testified that he had seen the shooting deaths of thousands of Jews, performed one at a time by a gunshot to the back of the head or to the neck:

> Even women carrying children two or three weeks old, sucking at their breasts, were not spared this horrible ordeal. Nor were mothers spared the terrible sight of their children being gripped by their little legs and put to death with one stroke of the pistol butt or club, thereafter to be thrown on the heap of human bodies in the ditch, some of which were not quite dead. Not before these mothers had been exposed to this worst of all tortures did they receive the bullet that released them from this sight.[37]

Every Jew in Uman was killed that day—an estimated 24,000 men, women, and children.

Two weeks later, the same soldiers—members of *Einsatzgruppe C*—rounded up Jews in the region around Kiev and marched them to the northwest sector of the city to a place known as Old Woman's Gully—in Russian, Babi Yar. There, on September 29 and 30, 1941, another 33,771 Jews were butchered. A German eyewitness, Fritz Höfer, testified that the Nazis and their Ukrainian collaborators again forced Jews—men, women, and children—to strip, abandon their possessions, and enter the ravine. Once in the ravine, Höfer stated, the Jews were "made to lie down on top of Jews who had already been shot. This all happened very quickly. The corpses were literally in layers. A police marksman came along and shot each Jew in the neck with a submachine gun at the spot where he was lying."[38]

After the massacre, Nazi soldiers covered the ravine with a thick layer of earth. A non-Jewish witness to the killings, Sergey Ivanovich Lutsenko, the cemetery's watchman, later testified that "the earth was moving long after, because wounded and still alive Jews were still moving [underneath the soil]."[39]

By December 1941, *Einsatzgruppe C*, under Brigadier General Otto Rasch, had murdered 95,000 people, including 75,000 Jews in the Kiev area. The other three units boasted similar numbers, but the psychological toll on soldiers in the *Einsatzgruppen* began to show. When Himmler visited one unit, the commander told him, "Look at the eyes of these men of this command, how deeply shaken they are. These men are finished for the rest of their lives."[40] Himmler personally witnessed one massacre, was sickened by it, but still supported the policy. Better methods, he felt, would have to be devised—less public, more cost-effective, and less traumatic for Nazi troops.

The Wannsee Conference

On January 20, 1942, at a conference in a western suburb of Berlin—in a posh villa on the shore of Lake Wannsee—15 men considered the best and brightest of the Reich met with Reinhard Heydrich to hear his report

A Survivor of the Babi Yar Massacre

One of the few Jews who survived the massacre at Babi Yar was Dina Pronicheva. Unlike most victims who had only been wounded before being thrown into the ravine, she miraculously avoided suffocation and managed to sneak away and hide in the woods after crawling out of the ravine. After the war, she spoke to a Russian writer, who related her story:

> All around and beneath her she could hear strange submerged sounds, groaning, choking and sobbing: many of the people were not dead yet. The whole mass of bodies kept moving slightly as they settled down and were pressed tighter by the movements of the ones who were still living. Some soldiers came out on to the ledge . . . firing bullets . . . into any which appeared to be still living. . . .
>
> A few minutes later . . . earth and sand landed on the bodies, coming closer and closer until it started falling on Dina herself. Her whole body was buried under the sand but she did not move until it began to cover her mouth. She was lying face upwards, breathed in some sand and started to choke, and then . . . she started scraping the sand off herself, scarcely daring to breathe lest she should start coughing. . . . Finally she got herself out from under the earth. . . . It was pitch dark and there was the heavy smell of flesh from the mass of fresh corpses.

Quoted in A. Anatoli (Kuznetsov), *Babi Yar: A Document in the Form of a Novel*. New York: Farrar, Straus and Giroux, 1970, pp. 110–11, 113.

outlining "The Final Solution." During the conference, Heydrich made clear that the Reich intended to exterminate as many as 11 million Jews in Europe, that he was in charge of the operation, and that he had specific ideas about how to accomplish that goal. Attendees at Wannsee heard that six extermination camps were either under construction or had recently been completed in the General Government. They were Treblinka, Belzec, Sobibór, Majdanek, Chelmno, and Auschwitz-Birkenau.

According to Martin Gilbert:

What had hitherto been tentative, fragmentary, and spasmodic was to become formal, comprehensive and efficient. The technical services such as railways, the bureaucracy and the diplomats would work in harmony, towards a single goal. . . . By the end of January 1942, the Germans needed only to establish the apparatus of total destruction: death camps in remote areas, rolling stock [trucks and trains], timetables, confiscation patterns, deportation schedules, and camps; and then to rely upon the tacit, unspoken, unrecorded connivance of thousands of people: administrators and bureaucrats who would do their duty, organize round-ups, supervise detention centres, coordinate schedules, and send local Jews on their way.[41]

Ten days after the Wannsee Conference, Hitler spoke at the Sports Palace in Berlin, saying, "The war will not end as the Jews imagine it will, namely, with the uprooting of the Aryans, but the result of this war will be the complete annihilation of the Jews."[42] As he spoke, millions of Jews in Polish ghettos were being told to prepare for deportation.

Deportation

Soon after Wannsee, officials in each ghetto—the *Judenrat*, or Jewish Council—received orders that they were to select individuals for transport to other camps in the east. These Jewish leaders were forced to select fellow Jews and have them gather at what one scholar calls every town's "starting point on the road to death"[43]—the train station.

Elie Wiesel describes the selection process that he witnessed:

> By eight o'clock in the morning, . . . there were shouts in the street. "All Jews outside! Hurry!". . . One by one the houses emptied, and the streets filled with people and bundles. By ten o'clock, all the condemned were outside. The police took a roll call, once, twice, twenty times. The heat was intense. Sweat streamed from faces and bodies. Children cried for water. Water? There was plenty, close at hand, in the houses, in the yards, but they were forbidden to break the ranks. . . . Then, at last, at one o'clock in the afternoon, came the signal to leave. . . . They began their journey without a backward glance at the abandoned streets, the dead, empty houses, the gardens, the tombstones. . . . On everyone's back was a pack. In everyone's eyes was suffering drowned in tears. Slowly, heavily, the procession made its way to the gate of the ghetto.[44]

Many Jews were told they were being relocated, but they seemed to know what lay ahead. They went anyway, because they felt they had nowhere to turn for help.

Once Jews left the ghetto, they were herded like animals into railroad cars and locked in. Each boxcar held 60 to 100 people. The cars were overcrowded, so prisoners had to take turns sitting down. Sometimes they were locked in without food, water, or toilets for a week or more. Many died. One transport took 27 days. When the boxcars were opened, no one had survived the trip. Those who survived other transports soon discovered they were not going to a better place. They were going to a death camp.

At the six Nazi death camps, 3 to 4 million people were murdered between 1942 and 1945. The camps were located in remote areas of Poland, to hide their purpose. The largest camp in size was Treblinka, but the most deadly was Auschwitz-Birkenau. Over 1 million people were killed there with poison gas and their bodies burned in crematory ovens. Nine out of 10 were Jews.

Hundreds of Hungarian Jews arrive at Auschwitz in 1945, the death camp in which the Nazis murdered more than a million Jews and others. The chimneys of the crematoria, where the bodies of the victims were burned, can be seen in the background.

Death Camps

Each time a trainload of Jews arrived at a concentration camp, the routine was the same. Once the bodies of those who had not survived the trip were removed, the other prisoners were ordered out of the boxcars to line up. Most stumbled out, too weak, hungry, and filthy to resist. Some did not realize what was about to happen. Others did. They had heard rumors of death camps where Jews were killed and their bodies burned. They saw smoke billowing from camp chimneys and smelled an odd, sickly sweet smell in the air. They knew they were about to die.

Nazi officials wanted the process to run smoothly. In most camps they made every effort to convince newly arrived Jews that they had

Killing Vans

I n addition to shooting individuals one at a time during Operation Barbarossa, one unit, *Einsatzgruppe D*, experimented with motorized gas chambers. Like the facilities that had been used in the T-4 euthanasia program, these vans, manufactured by the Saurer Corporation of Berlin, killed with carbon monoxide gas. They resembled closed trucks, and as they were driven, exhaust gases piped into the body of the van caused death in 10 to 15 minutes. The driver's compartment, of course, was sealed off from the main compartment. Vans of this type were also used at Chelmno, the first of the Nazi extermination camps, opened in December 1941 near Lodz. In all, gas vans were used to kill 500,000 people, primarily Jews.

Otto Ohlendorf, commander of *Einsatzgruppe D*, complained about the early vans, saying victims often defecated and urinated during their death throes, leaving a filthy mess for his men to have to deal with. His men also complained about headaches from the fumes. The inventor of the vans, SS Lieutenant August Becker, adjusted the rate at which the gas was released, allowing victims to first pass out before lethal levels were reached. The results were encouraging, but in the end, the vehicles were deemed inadequate for mass murder on the scale necessary to accomplish Hitler's goal of a Jew-free Europe.

come to a new work camp. The train stations looked like those in small towns across Germany and Poland. One survivor, Tadeusz Borowski, later described the Auschwitz railroad station as "a cheerful little station, very much like any other provincial railway stop: a small square framed by tall chestnuts [trees] and paved with yellow gravel."[45]

Some camps welcomed new arrivals with a band playing classical music. Others put up signs labeled "Tailors," "Carpenters," and other professions, to make prisoners think there was work for them. In other camps Nazis did not use such tricks. Instead, they used brute force—snarling dogs, shouted commands, whips, and clubs—to enforce order.

In each camp, no matter how they had been greeted, Jews were forced to go through another selection. This time, Nazis separated men from women and children. The stronger men were put to work in the camp's factories. The older men, most of the women, and all the younger children were sent directly to "showers" to clean up. To those who did not know what lay in store, a shower sounded wonderful after such a grueling trip, so they went willingly. Others who had guessed that "showers" were actually disguised gas chambers usually followed meekly, too weak to resist.

One Holocaust survivor, Ernst Michel, describes what happened when he arrived at Auschwitz and came face to face with the officer in charge of selection, Josef Mengele:

> We were forced into two columns, women on one side, men on the other side. . . . At the end of the line there was an SS man in a beautiful leather coat [Mengele], and as we walked by he asked us, "How old?" If you were between the ages of sixteen and thirty, the thumb went up and you went to one side. Over thirty, the thumb went down, and you went to the other side. . . . They piled us into trucks, and then a guard said something to me that I didn't understand. He said, "You're the lucky ones." I said, "What do you mean?" And he said, "The others are already up the chimney." That's when we started to realize what this place was.[46]

The Showers

Even in buildings disguised as showers, the Nazis tried to fool victims into thinking everything was going to be all right. In dressing rooms, guards told them to undress, hang their clothes on numbered hooks (so they would be able to find them afterward), and take soap and a towel. In some camps, as many as 2,000 Jews at a time were then herded into vast rooms with showerheads in the ceilings.

Once the doors were closed and sealed, however, no water came through the showerheads. And the floors had no drains. Instead, poison gas poured in—produced when the bluish hydrogen cyanide pellets known commercially as Zyklon B were poured through small rooftop openings into the gas chambers below. Within three to five minutes, each man, woman, and child in the room was dead. In 1942 Auschwitz alone used 8.2 tons of Zyklon B. In 1943 it used 13.4 tons.

When cyanide fumes had cleared the gas chambers, other camp prisoners entered the room to remove the dead. They shaved the heads of the dead and searched the mouths for gold teeth. The hair would later be used as insulation in German submarines or made into liners for

Piles of hair shaved from the heads of murdered Jews offer a stark reminder of the evils committed by Adolf Hitler and his Nazi regime. The Germans used the hair as insulation in submarines and as liners for felt boots.

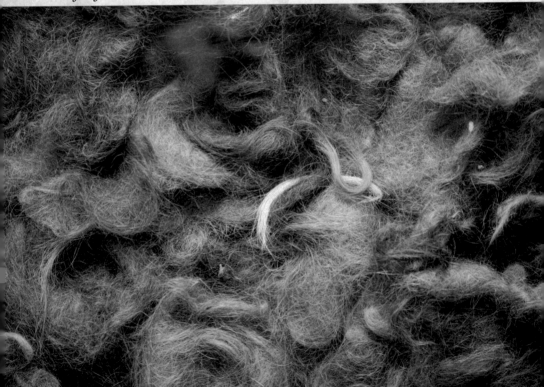

felt boots. The gold from teeth would be melted down and poured into gold bars. At Auschwitz, prisoners collected about 100 pounds (45.4 kg) of gold for the Nazis each day. Finally, workers carried or dragged the dead to huge pits for burial or to one of several crematories—special ovens where they were burned to ash. This assembly-line process was efficient. In Auschwitz, for example, Nazi officials boasted they could process 12,000 victims per day. By early 1943 four state-of-the-art gas chamber/crematory installations were at work in Auschwitz-Birkenau, the Reich's top killing center.

"The Lucky Ones"

About 80 percent of the Jews arriving at Auschwitz went directly to the gas chambers. Those "lucky ones" the concentration guard mentioned—the few prisoners who survived the selection at the train station—went to long buildings where guards took away their possessions. They shaved their heads, gave them striped prison uniforms, and at some camps tattooed numbers on their arms. Primo Levi, an Italian survivor of Auschwitz, later wrote about the experience: "Nothing belongs to us any more; they have taken away our clothes, our shoes, even our hair; if we speak, they will not listen to us, and if they listen, they will not understand. They will even take away our name."[47]

Before dawn each morning, a whistle blew, telling prisoners they had 30 minutes to dress, wash, and eat breakfast. Most slept in their clothes, since few had blankets. Washing was difficult because hundreds in each barracks shared only a few faucets. Breakfast was usually a piece of bread and sometimes a pint of thin broth.

Everyone then went to roll call in the camp's central area. This often took an hour, during which they were not allowed to move. Guards wanted to assure themselves that no one had tried to escape during the night and to count prisoners who had died in their bunks overnight. Roll call was a dangerous time. Sometimes officers selected weaker inmates and sent them to the gas chambers. Many times during roll call, Nazi guards shot prisoners for minor offenses such as not standing at attention.

If prisoners survived roll call, they went to work. Those with special skills—machine operators, steel workers, electricians, etc.—went to the camp factories. Others worked in rock quarries, the camp kitchen, or the laundry. Some helped build barracks. Some spent their days sorting through mountains of suitcases, clothing, eyeglasses, jewelry, and shoes taken from victims of the gas chambers. Some helped process those victims, pulling their bodies out of the gas chambers, searching them, or carrying them to the ovens or to burial pits.

In the evening, after a long day of backbreaking work and little rest, they marched back to their barracks for another roll call, again lasting over an hour. During this roll call, all were ordered to remain in line until any missing prisoners were found. Once, at Buchenwald, prisoners had to remain in line at evening roll call for 19 hours, until two men who had tried to hide were found.

End of the Line

Hard work, little food, cruel treatment, and extreme temperatures soon took their toll. In most camps, few workers lasted more than a few months before becoming too weak to continue. When that happened, they usually marched to their deaths without resistance.

Mass murder in Nazi death camps continued unabated from 1942 to 1945. In the final months of the war, however, Allied troops driving the Nazis out of previously occupied territories began to discover the abandoned camps. What they saw shocked the world.

Chapter 5

What Is the Legacy of the Holocaust?

A few reports hinting at what was happening inside Nazi death camps leaked to the outside world during the war. Some came from non-Jewish families who lived near the camps and wrote to relatives about what they had observed. Others came from those few Jews who had escaped. Most people who heard these reports, however, dismissed them, believing that such horrific tales could not possibly be true. They felt they must have been exaggerated anti-Nazi propaganda.

The world outside the Third Reich did not fully comprehend the true horrors of the Holocaust until the final months of World War II, when Allied troops began liberating the camps and reporting what they saw. Likewise, the outside world did not learn until after the war of the heroism of Jewish resistance fighters in some ghettos and camps or of those brave non-Jewish civilians who helped hide Jews from the Nazis or helped them to escape.

With defeat imminent, Adolf Hitler committed suicide in his Berlin bunker on April 30, 1945. Reich officials surrendered two days later, ending the war in Europe. Once the war was over, the Allies faced several daunting problems. First, they needed to save as many Jewish prisoners as possible. They also had to decide what to do with Nazi officers and soldiers who had committed such horrible acts. Finally, they wanted to help Jews restart their lives and to provide a safe place for them to live. Jews and non-Jews around the world also faced tasks: to honor those who had fought to save victims of the Holocaust, to memorialize those who had perished at the hands of the Nazis, and to ensure that the horrors of the Holocaust would never be forgotten.

Nazi Desperation

By late 1944 Soviet troops were advancing on Germany from the east. British, Canadian, French, and American troops were moving in from the west and south. Despite their military defeats, however, the Nazis were determined to continue killing Jews. When it became obvious their troops would have to retreat into Germany from occupied territories, these same officials ordered camps in Poland torn down.

They wanted to destroy evidence of what they had been doing. In addition to destroying camp buildings, Nazis ordered the remaining

Allied troops, advancing into territories formerly controlled by Germany, encountered many gruesome sights. At the Bergen-Belsen concentration camp in Germany (pictured here in May 1945), they found open pits filled with the skeleton-like remains of victims of the Nazis.

bodies of victims burned. They ordered thousands of bodies that had been buried earlier in mass graves to be dug up and burned. Once this was accomplished, they ordered grass planted on the burial pits, hoping to disguise them. They also forced remaining prisoners to march hundreds of miles through snow back to Germany. On these death marches, tens of thousands died—frozen, starved, or shot along the way. Their bodies were left to rot alongside roadways.

Despite their efforts, Nazis could not hide all they had done at the death camps. Units of the Soviet army moved swiftly into eastern Poland in the summer of 1944. Near the Polish city of Lublin, Soviet troops liberated the first of these camps—Majdanek—freeing the few survivors still there. A few months later, on January 27, 1945, Soviets reached Auschwitz. They found the burning ruins of camp buildings. They also discovered, wandering amid the ruins, 7,000 live inmates in a camp where more than 1 million human beings had been murdered.

Liberation and Witness

As Allied forces advanced on Berlin, Nazi concentration camps in Germany and Nazi-occupied Western Europe were discovered. On April 11, 1945, American forces entered two of the worst camps in Germany—Buchenwald, near Weimar, and the Nordhausen Dora-Mittelbau complex, 45 miles (72.4 km) to the northwest. At those camps and at many others, US soldiers came face to face with mounds of dead bodies, instruments of Nazi torture, and thousands of prisoners who were barely alive. Battle-hardened soldiers were horrified by the sights.

Major Haynes Dugan, public affairs officer of the US 3rd Armored "Spearhead" Division, later reported what he saw when he entered Nordhausen:

Although the taking of Nordhausen did not constitute the heaviest fighting of April 11, that city will live forever in the memories of 3rd Armored Division soldiers as a place of horror. . . . No written word can properly convey the atmosphere of such a charnel house [slaughterhouse], the unbearable stench of decomposing bodies, the sight of human beings, starved to pallid skeletons, lying cheek to jowl with the ten-day dead.

Hundreds of corpses lay sprawled over the acres of the big compound. More hundreds filled the great barracks. They lay in contorted heaps, half stripped, mouths gaping in the dirt and straw; or, they were piled naked, like cordwood, in the corners and under the stairways.

Everywhere among the dead were the living emaciated, ragged shapes whose fever-bright eyes waited passively for the release of death. Over all the area clung the terrible odor of decomposition and, like a dirge of forlorn hope, the combined cries of these unfortunates rose and fell in weak undulations. It was a fabric of moans and whimpers, of delirium and outright madness. Here and there a single shape tottered about, walking slowly, like a man dreaming.[48]

On April 15, British forces came upon Bergen-Belsen. There they found so many unburied bodies that they were forced to use a bulldozer to bury them. To document what they witnessed, British officials filmed the operation. That black-and-white footage still shocks students of the Holocaust.

Another camp liberated by Allied troops was Dachau, the first camp built by the Nazis. Jack Hallett, one of the US soldiers who helped liberate that camp on April 29, later spoke of his experience:

The first thing I saw was a stack of bodies that appeared to be about, oh, twenty feet long and about, oh, as high as a man could reach, which looked like cordwood stacked up there, and the thing I'll never forget was the fact that closer inspection found people whose eyes were still blinking maybe three for four deep inside the stack.[49]

What Hallett described was the shocking revelation that prisoners who were still alive but too weak to move had been stacked among the dead.

Evidence of the Slaughter at Auschwitz

Nazi guards at Auschwitz tried to destroy what possessions they had taken from the 1.1 million Jews they had murdered there, but they could not destroy all the evidence. When the camp was liberated in 1945, Soviet soldiers found buildings containing 830,000 women's coats and dresses, 348,000 men's suits, 38,000 pairs of men's shoes, and seven tons of human hair. Laurence Rees, author of *Auschwitz: A New History*, related the testimony of one survivor of Auschwitz who bore witness to the scope of destruction at that camp, specifically to the murder of 200,000 children within its walls:

> One image stuck in my mind from the moment I [Rees] heard it described. It was of a "procession" of empty baby carriages—property looted from the dead Jews—pushed out of Auschwitz in rows of five towards the railway station. The prisoner who witnessed the sight said they took an hour to pass by.

Laurence Rees, *Auschwitz: A New History*. New York: PublicAffairs, 2005, p. xxi.

Caring for the Living

At every camp, the Allies' first task was to provide immediate care for starving prisoners. They provided fresh water for drinking and bathing. They brought in truckloads of food, but many Jews were too weak to eat. Some ate too much and died as a result. Their digestive systems could not take solid food after so long on starvation rations. Doctors and nurses did what they could, but in the following weeks, thousands more died.

When former prisoners eventually regained their strength, they wanted to go home. Many, however, had no home to return to. Joshua

M. Greene and Shiva Kumar, editors of *Witness: Voices from the Holocaust*, write:

> Those still alive among the victimized had to redefine the meaning of freedom in a world where their families, their homes, and their towns, villages, and religious communities had been destroyed forever.
>
> For those who survived the camps and death marches, "liberation" offered little solace. Most were alone. They were ill, weak, and malnourished, facing a bleak and uncertain future. Those of us who today celebrate the "triumph of survival" overlook the burden of survivors' painful memories and their sense at liberation that "I'm not alive, I'm dead" and "I'm alive, but so what?"[50]

Many of the 250,000 Jews who were classified as Displaced Persons, or DPs, had to stay in special camps set up for them by Allied soldiers. Eventually, most were resettled. Many settled in the United States, Western Europe, South America, Australia, and South Africa. Others moved to British-controlled Palestine, in the Middle East.

Around the world, people who learned of the Holocaust felt shame and guilt that something like this could have happened. Sympathy for Europe's Jewish survivors led nations to call for the establishment of a Jewish homeland in Palestine. With help from the newly organized United Nations, Israel became an independent nation on May 14, 1948, and welcomed thousands of European Jews.

The State of Israel

Harry S. Truman, US president at the end of World War II, favored a separate Jewish state in Palestine. According to biographer David McCullough:

> Truman felt pulled in several directions. Like the great majority of Americans, he wanted to do what was right for the hundreds of thousands of European Jews, survivors of the Holocaust,

who had suffered such unimaginable horrors. His sympathy for them was heartfelt and deep-seated. As senator, at [a] mass meeting in Chicago in 1943, he had said everything "humanly possible" must be done to provide a haven for Jewish survivors of the Nazis.[51]

In 1945 Truman sent Earl G. Harrison, dean of the University of Pennsylvania Law School and former US commissioner of immigration, to Europe to investigate the Displaced Persons camps and interview occupants. Harrison's report to Truman made clear his belief that only in a separate homeland in Palestine would Jews "be welcomed and find peace and quiet and be given the opportunity to live and work."[52]

On April 2, 1947, Great Britain officially requested that the United Nations General Assembly establish the Special Committee on Palestine (UNSCOP). The committee eventually recommended that Palestine be partitioned into two states. With strong support from the United States, UN Resolution 181—creating separate Jewish and Palestinian homelands, with an international zone around Jerusalem—passed.

A rabbi in the delegates' lounge at the UN rejoiced, "This is the day the Lord hath made!" Abba Eban, who later became a prominent Israeli diplomat, attended the vote at the United Nations. When the results were announced, he recalls, "there were Jews in tears, and non-Jews moved by the nobility of the occasion. Nobody who ever lived that moment will ever lose its memory from his heart."[53]

At midnight on May 14, 1948, David Ben-Gurion, the first prime minister of the Provisional Government of Israel, read aloud that nation's "Declaration of Independence," proclaiming the existence of the new State of Israel. That same day, President Truman, acting for the United States, officially recognized the Provisional Government as the legitimate authority of the new Jewish state. Arabs in the region were incensed and launched the first Arab-Israeli War, which lasted less than one year and resulted in armistices between Israel and several Arab nations.

The 1948-1949 conflict was the first in a series of armed disputes between Israel and its Arab neighbors. During the Six-Day War in June

A Legacy of Tolerance Versus a Legacy of Hate

The Southern Poverty Law Center in Birmingham, Alabama, is an organization dedicated to monitoring discrimination in the United States. Its website contains information about US hate groups. One feature, the Hate Map, shows known neo-Nazi groups scattered across the country. These groups are made up of members who believe Adolf Hitler and his policy of annihilation of Jews was the right thing to do. Looking at the number of swastikas on the Hate Map, each representing such a group, is a chilling reminder that Hitler's influence did not end with his death.

The swastika, of course, was the symbol of Nazi Germany, and its presence in so many areas of a current US map is one hint of the alarming growth of neo-Nazi groups in the United States and Europe. A member of one such group, in the summer of 2009, came to the United States Holocaust Memorial Museum in Washington, DC, intent on killing as many of its visitors as he could. Only the self-sacrifice of a security guard at the museum, Stephen Tyrone Johns, prevented the bloodshed. This neo-Nazi attacker (whose name need not be remembered) had been indoctrinated to hate Jews. His assault on the museum's visitors was his way of expressing this rabid anti-Semitism.

1967 and the 1973 Yom Kippur War, Israeli troops defeated their enemies, gaining territory for Israel. Prospects for lasting peace have risen and fallen over time, but conflict and animosity between Arabs and Israelis still exist. Some scholars believe the State of Israel would never have been established had the Holocaust not occurred. Others feel its creation was inevitable. Whatever the case, Israel's continued existence provides Jews a homeland and the means to ensure that such large-scale, government-sanctioned persecution of Jews cannot happen again.

Justice and Retribution

While former concentration camp prisoners were being cared for and resettled, and while world powers were debating the creation of the State of Israel, the Allies focused on seeking justice for Holocaust victims. In war, death and suffering are expected. What the Nazis had done went far beyond the normal scope of war. It was a crime, and the world demanded justice. Hitler had killed himself, but many Nazi officers and soldiers who had participated in the Holocaust were captured. On October 6, 1945, war crimes trials began in Nuremberg, Germany.

Three classifications of crimes were listed in the charges read at the trials. Some were charged with crimes against peace—planning, preparing, and waging a war that violated earlier treaties. Others were charged with war crimes—mistreating, torturing, or enslaving civilians and prisoners of war, and destroying cities and towns that had no military purpose. Most, though, were charged with crimes against humanity—murdering, mistreating, torturing, or enslaving civilians for religious, racial, or political reasons.

All but one Nazi defendant at the first Nuremberg trial pleaded *nicht schuldig* ("not guilty"), saying they were just following orders. When the trial was over, thirteen were sentenced to death, three to life in prison, and four to long prison terms. Three were found not guilty. Hermann Göring, condemned to hang for his crimes, managed to commit suicide before his sentence could be carried out. Between 1945 and 1949, 12 additional trials held Nazis accountable for their crimes. The commandant of Auschwitz, Rudolf Höss, was arrested in 1946. At his trial in Warsaw, Poland, in April 1947, and to his last breath before being executed, Höss maintained that what he had done—helping to implement Hitler's Final Solution—had been "right."[54]

After the Nuremberg trials, other Nazis who escaped Germany at the end of the war were hunted down and put on trial. Nazi-hunters such as Simon Wiesenthal, a survivor of Buchenwald and several other concentration camps, devoted their lives to bringing Nazi war criminals to justice. The search for Nazi war criminals continues to this day.

Remembrance

World War II in Europe was over. Survivors had been cared for. New homes had been found for them. Many Nazis responsible for the deaths of millions had been brought to justice. All that remained was to memorialize the dead, honor those who had done what they could to save victims of Nazi cruelty, and make sure the world never forgot the Holocaust.

Philosopher and historian George Santayana once wrote, "Those who cannot remember the past are condemned to repeat it."[55] If future generations do not learn about what the Nazis did to the Jews and to others, it could happen again. To prevent that from happening, many nations have built monuments devoted to the Holocaust. Memorials have been built on the sites of some concentration camps in Germany and Poland. Israel opened its national Holocaust center, Yad Vashem, on a Jerusalem hillside in 1953. In addition to museums and memorials, Yad Vashem also contains a research center for studying Jewish culture, the victims of the Holocaust, and heroes of the Jewish resistance. Israel also honors those it calls "The Righteous"—non-Jews who helped Jews escape the horrors of the Holocaust.

When Hitler first came to power in Germany and began his program to rid the country of Jews, some German citizens defied the new laws. They continued to shop in Jewish-owned stores. Some took Jewish families into their homes to hide them from the Nazis. Others tried to smuggle Jews out of the country. Once Germany had taken over most of Eastern Europe, citizens of some occupied countries also worked to save as many Jews as they could. Some of the non-Jews who sacrificed to save Jews—people like Oskar Schindler, whose actions were immortalized in the book and movie *Schindler's List*—have been honored for their courage by being named "Righteous Among the Nations" by Holocaust survivors.

More than any other Holocaust memorial in the world today, the United States Holocaust Memorial Museum, which opened its doors in Washington, DC, in 1993, brings the memory of the Holocaust to life. Films, audio recordings, computer programs, actual buildings from the era, photographs, and artifacts from the camps help re-create the

Jews who survived starvation and torture pose for their liberators at a concentration camp in Austria in May 1945. In the years that followed, survivors and others documented for all the world the horrors of the Holocaust.

Holocaust experience for museum visitors. At its dedication ceremony, Holocaust survivor Elie Wiesel said: "For the dead and the living, we must bear witness. For not only are we responsible for the memories of the dead, we are also responsible for what we are doing with those memories. . . . We could not save those who died, but we can save them from dying again, because to forget is to kill them again."[56]

In addition to museums and memorials, some survivors and their children have formed organizations to keep the memory alive. In June 1981, for example, more than 6,000 survivors from around the globe met in Jerusalem. Organizations in the United States like the American Gathering of Jewish Holocaust Survivors and One Generation After sponsor meetings and special events to commemorate the Holocaust.

A national holiday in Israel—Yad Hashoah, Holocaust Day of Remembrance—honors those who died and those who risked their lives to save them.

Witnesses

Two victims of Nazi Germany—both classified by Hitler as "enemies of the state"—survived the Reich's prison camps and today offer poignant descriptions of the Holocaust. The first, Martin Niemoller, was a prominent Protestant theologian and minister in Germany before World War II. Arrested for his opposition to Nazi policy in 1937, he spent the war in various concentration camps. After the war he toured the United States, bringing a message of concern for others. His often-quoted statement ruefully confesses his initial indifference toward the fate of Jews and others targeted by Nazi Germany:

> First they came for the Communists, and I did not speak out—because I was not a Communist;
>
> Then they came for the Socialists, and I did not speak out—because I was not a Socialist;
>
> Then they came for the trade unionists, and I did not speak out—because I was not a trade unionist;
>
> Then they came for the Jews, and I did not speak out—because I was not a Jew;
>
> Then they came for me—and there was no one left to speak out for me.[57]

The second witness, Hugo Gabriel Gryn, was liberated from Auschwitz in 1945 at the age of 15. His father survived the horrors of the camp with him, only to die in his son's arms hours after their liberation. Gryn later immigrated to England and served as rabbi for one of the largest Jewish congregations in Europe until his death in 1996. To Gryn, the Holocaust was "a denial of God. It was a denial of man. It was the destruction of the world in miniature form."[58]

Never Forget

Today, some people claim the Holocaust never happened—that the camps were never used for the annihilation of an entire people, that millions were never gassed and that their bodies were never incinerated, that they were simply prisoners of war who died from natural causes. Those who deny the Holocaust claim that the horror stories told by survivors are exaggerations or outright lies.

A multitude of evidence exists, however. For most, it is impossible to ignore. For those who did not live through the Holocaust—who did not see its horrors firsthand—its impact will depend upon preserving that evidence, remembering what happened, and never forgetting those who died.

Source Notes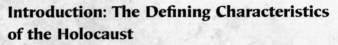

Introduction: The Defining Characteristics of the Holocaust

1. Elie Wiesel, *Night*. New York: Bantam, published by arrangement with Hill & Wang, 1960, p. 109.
2. Elie Wiesel, *Night*, p. 32.
3. *Merriam-Webster OnLine Dictionary*, s.v. "holocaust." www.merriam-webster.com.
4. United States Holocaust Memorial Museum, "The Holocaust." www.ushmm.org.
5. Quoted in John Toland, *Adolf Hitler*. Garden City, NY: Doubleday, 1976, p. 122n.

Chapter One: What Conditions Led to the Holocaust?

6. Martin Luther, *On the Jews and Their Lies*. Wittenberg, Germany, 1543. www.humanitas-international.org.
7. Ronald Berger, *Fathoming the Holocaust: A Social Problems Approach*. New York: Aldine de Gruyter, 2002, p. 28.
8. Martin Gilbert, *The Holocaust: A History of the Jews of Europe During the Second World War*. New York: Holt, Rinehart and Winston, 1985, p. 20.
9. Gilbert, *The Holocaust*, pp. 21–22.
10. Chaim Weizmann, "Letter 44," in *The Letters and Papers of Chaim Weizmann*, vol. IX, series A, October 1918–July 1920, ed. Jehuda Reinharz. Jerusalem, Israel: Israel Universities, 1977, p. 48.
11. Quoted in Robert Ley, ed., "Document No. 1708-PS," Avalon Project: Documents in Law, History, and Diplomacy, Yale University Law Library. avalon.law.yale.edu.

Chapter Two: Prelude to Annihilation

12. Michael Berenbaum, foreword, to *The Holocaust Chronicle: A History in Words and Pictures,* edited by David J. Hogan. Lincolnwood, IL: Publications International, 2001, p. 11.

13. Sara J. Bloomfield, "A Time to Confront Hate: Officer's Legacy at Holocaust Museum," *USA Today,* June 24, 2009. usatoday.com.

14. Quoted in Eric A. Johnson and Karl-Heinz Reuband, *What We Knew: Terror, Mass Murder, and Everyday Life in Nazi Germany; An Oral History.* Cambridge, MA: Basic Books, 2005, pp. 26–27.

15. Quoted in David M. Dickerson, "The Third Reich: Wehrmacht Oath of Loyalty," Institute for Global Communication. ddickerson.igc.org.

16. Quoted in Joshua M. Greene and Shiva Kumar, eds., *Witness: Voices from the Holocaust.* New York: Free Press, 2000, p. 14.

17. Quoted in Hogan, *The Holocaust Chronicle*, p. 103.

18. Hogan, *The Holocaust Chronicle*, p. 123.

19. Quoted in Gilbert, *The Holocaust*, p. 71.

20. Quoted in Gilbert, *The Holocaust*, p. 71.

21. Quoted in Johnson and Reuband, *What We Knew*, pp. 35–36.

22. Quoted in Johnson and Reuband, *What We Knew*, p. 45.

Chapter Three: The Road to Auschwitz

23. Quoted in Ian Kershaw, *Hitler, the Germans and the Final Solution.* Jerusalem, and New Haven, CT: International Institute for Holocaust Research and Yale University Press, 2008, pp. 103–4.

24. Gilbert, *The Holocaust*, p. 87.

25. Laurence Rees, *Auschwitz: A New History.* New York: PublicAffairs, 2005, p. 13.

26. Quoted in Christopher R. Browning, "Before the Final Solution: Nazi Ghettoization Policy in Poland (1940–1941)," in *Ghettos 1939–1945: New Research and Perspectives on Definition, Daily Life, and Survival; Symposium Presentations.* Washington, DC: Center for Advanced Holocaust Studies, United States Holocaust Memorial Museum, 2005, p. 14. www.ushmm.org.

27. Quoted in Greene and Kumar, *Witness: Voices from the Holocaust*, p. 47.

28. Quoted in S.L. Schneiderman, ed., *Warsaw Ghetto: A Diary by Mary Berg*. New York: L.B. Fischer, 1945, p. 20.

29. Quoted in Green and Kumar, *Witness: Voices from the Holocaust*, p. 67.

30. Quoted in Mark P. Mostert, "Useless Eaters: Disability as Genocidal Marker in Nazi Germany," *Journal of Special Education*, vol. 36, no. 3, 2002, p. 157. www.regent.edu.

31. Quoted in Hogan, *The Holocaust Chronicle*, p. 169.

32. United States Holocaust Memorial Museum, *Holocaust Encyclopedia*, "Concentration Camps, 1933–1939." www.ushmm.org.

33. Hogan, *The Holocaust Chronicle*, p. 186.

34. Rees, *Auschwitz: A New History*, p. 1.

Chapter Four: Mass Murder

35. Quoted in Kershaw, *Hitler, the Germans and the Final Solution*, p. 66.

36. Hogan, *The Holocaust Chronicle*, p. 212.

37. Quoted in Robert Edwin Herzstein and the Editors of Time-Life Books, *The Nazis*. New York: Time-Life, 1980, p. 142.

38. Quoted in Hogan, *The Holocaust Chronicle*, p. 211.

39. Quoted in Gilbert, *The Holocaust*, p. 203.

40. Quoted in Herzstein and the Editors of Time-Life Books, *The Nazis*, p. 142.

41. Gilbert, *The Holocaust*, pp. 283–84.

42. Foreign Broadcasting Monitoring Service, Federal Communications Commission, "Text of Speech by Chancellor Adolf Hitler at Berlin Sports Palace," January 30, 1942. www.ibiblio.org.

43. Johnson and Reuband, *What We Knew*, p. 365.

44. Wiesel, *Night*, pp. 13–14.

45. Quoted in Otto Friedrich, *The Kingdom of Auschwitz*. New York: HarperCollins, 1982, p. 20.

46. Quoted in Peter Jennings and Todd Brewster, *The Century*. New York: Doubleday, 1998, p. 265.

47. Quoted in Friedrich, *The Kingdom of Auschwitz*, p. 35.

Chapter Five: What Is the Legacy of the Holocaust?

48. Quoted in Michael Hirsh, *The Liberators: America's Witnesses to the Holocaust*. New York: Bantam, 2010, pp. 56–57.
49. Quoted in Robert H. Abzug, *Inside the Vicious Heart*. New York: Oxford University Press, 1985, p. 92.
50. Greene and Kumar, *Witness: Voices from the Holocaust*, p. 197.
51. David McCullough, *Truman*. New York: Simon & Schuster, 1992, p. 595.
52. Quoted in McCullough, *Truman*, p. 595.
53. Quoted in McCullough, *Truman*, p. 602.
54. Quoted in Rees, *Auschwitz: A New History*, p. 200.
55. Quoted in John Bartlett, *Familiar Quotations*. Boston: Little, Brown, 1968, p. 867.
56. Elie Wiesel, in *The Holocaust: In Memory of Millions*, documentary film, Discovery Productions, 1993.
57. Quoted in Franklin H. Littell, "First They Came for the Jews," *Christian Ethics Today*, vol. 3, no.9, February 1997, updated May 27, 2001. www.christianethicstoday.com.
58. Quoted in Michael Smith, "It Was an Evil So Monstrous That It Denied Belief," *Daily Telegraph* (London), January 27, 2001. www.telegraph.co.uk.

Important People of the Holocaust

Mordecai Anielewicz (1919–1943): Polish Jew who led the most successful organized Jewish resistance against Nazi armed forces during the Warsaw ghetto uprising (April 19–May 16, 1943).

Adolf Eichmann (1906–1962): Head of the Office of Jewish Emigration and the Reich's Jewish expert; architect of much of the Holocaust.

Anne Frank (1929–1945): A German Jewish girl whose family hid from the Nazis for over two years in a secret apartment above a factory in Amsterdam, Netherlands. Her diary was discovered after the war by her father and became an international bestseller, *Anne Frank: The Diary of a Young Girl*.

Joseph Goebbels (1897–1945): Nazi propaganda minister for the Third Reich.

Hermann Göring (1893–1946): Second in power only to Hitler in the Third Reich; commander in chief of the *Luftwaffe*, the German air force.

Reinhard Heydrich (1904–1942): Head of Germany's Central Security Office; responsible for ordering that Jews be sent to ghettos.

Heinrich Himmler (1900–1945): Head of the SS.

Adolf Hitler (1889–1945): Head of the Nazi Party, author of *Mein Kampf*, chancellor and then dictator of Germany; absolute ruler of the Third Reich; mastermind of the Holocaust.

Rudolf Höss (1900–1947): Commandant of Auschwitz.

Martin Luther (1483–1546): German theologian and priest famous for instigating the Protestant Reformation in 1517; author of anti-Semitic treatise *On the Jews and Their Lies*.

Josef Mengele (1911–1979): SS member and camp doctor at Auschwitz; nicknamed "The Angel of Death" by inmates for his role in camp selections for the gas chamber and for inhuman medical experiments; eluded capture after the war and lived out his life in South America.

Ernst Röhm (1887–1934): Head of the SA; ordered killed because Hitler felt he was a potential threat to his rule.

Oskar Schindler (1908–1974): Polish businessman who built a factory in which he employed over one thousand Jewish workers, saving them from deportation to Nazi death camps.

Raoul Wallenberg (1912–1947?): Swedish diplomat, who came to Hungary and saved tens of thousands of Jews by passing out Swedish passports, providing shelter, food, and medicine. In 1945 he was accused of espionage by the Soviet Union and arrested. Soviet officials reported that Wallenberg died of a heart attack in a Soviet prison in 1947, but that has never been confirmed.

Elie Wiesel (1928–): Hungarian American Holocaust survivor; Nobel Peace Prize winner; author of numerous books on the Holocaust, including *Night*, his autobiographical account of life in Nazi concentration camps.

For Further Research

Books

Michael Berenbaum, *The World Must Know: The History of the Holocaust in the United States Holocaust Memorial Museum*. Baltimore: Johns Hopkins University Press, 2005.

Joshua M. Greene and Shiva Kumar, eds. *Witness: Voices from the Holocaust*. New York: Free Press, 2000.

Michael Hirsh, *The Liberators: America's Witnesses to the Holocaust*. New York: Bantam, 2010.

David J. Hogan, ed., *The Holocaust Chronicle: A History in Words and Pictures*. Lincolnwood, IL: Publications International, 2001.

Eric A. Johnson, *Nazi Terror: The Gestapo, Jews, and Ordinary Germans*. New York: Basic Books, 2000.

Eric A. Johnson and Karl-Heinz Reuband, *What We Knew: Terror, Mass Murder, and Everyday Life in Nazi Germany; An Oral History*. New York: Basic Books, 2005.

Ian Kershaw, *Hitler, the Germans, and the Final Solution*. Jerusalem: International Institute for Holocaust Research, 2008.

Primo Levi, *If This Is a Man*. New York: Everyman's Library, 2000. Originally published in Italy in 1958.

Laurence Rees, *Aushwitz: A New History*. New York: PublicAffairs, 2005.

Art Spiegelman, *Maus: A Survivor's Tale*. Vols. 1 and 2. New York: Pantheon, 1991.

Elie Wiesel, *After the Darkness: Reflections on the Holocaust*. New York: Schocken, 2002.

————, *Night*. Rev. Ed. New York: Hill and Wang, 2006. First published in France in 1958.

Websites:

Auschwitz-Birkenau Memorial and Museum (English version) (en. auschwitz.org.pl/z/index.php?option=com_content&task=view&id=6 &Itemid=8). Virtual tours of Auschwitz and Auschwitz II–Birkenau.

The Buchenwald and Mittelbau-Dora Memorials Foundation (www. buchenwald.de/index_en.html). The official website of Buchenwald, with virtual tours of both camps and the museum. Established in 2003 in Weimar, Germany.

"The Final Solution (The Holocaust, The Shoah)" (www.the-map-as-history.com/demos/tome08/05a-final_solution_holocaust_demo. php). An animated map with audio information, showing the progression of the Final Solution. Provides a four- to five-minute summary of the Holocaust. A production of Images et Savoirs, France.

The Fortunoff Video Archive for Holocaust Testimonies (www.li brary.yale.edu/testimonies). An archive with 4,400 videotaped interviews with Holocaust survivors and others with personal experience of the time. Sponsored by Yale University, New Haven, Connecticut.

"The Holocaust: A Tragic Legacy" (library.thinkquest.org/12663). An interactive site designed by students that provides background information, a Holocaust timeline, glossary, audio testimonies of camp survivors, and quizzes of Holocaust knowledge.

The Holocaust Chronicle (www.holocaustchronicle.org). An online version of a print encyclopedia of the Holocaust. Thousands of facts, images, and maps searchable by date, keyword, or chapter.

The Holocaust Cybrary (remember.org). A link page to virtual tours of concentration camps, images of the camps during the Holocaust and now, and other resources. A project of the Alliance for a Better Earth, Groveton, Georgia.

The Holocaust/Shoah Page (frank.mtsu.edu/~baustin/holo.html). Links to articles, images, etc., about the Holocaust. Sponsored by the Holocaust Studies Committee at Middle Tennessee State University, Murfreesboro, Tennessee.

The Nizkor Project (www.nizkor.org/index.html). Links to books, picture collections, maps, etc., about the Holocaust.

The United States Holocaust Memorial Museum (www.ushmm.org). A virtual tour of the largest Holocaust museum in the world. Contains thousands of images, recorded interviews with camp survivors, and a research center with unmatched resources.

USC Shoah Foundation Institute for Visual History and Education (college.usc.edu/vhi). An extensive library of video interviews of Holocaust survivors, liberators, and others involved in the Holocaust.

"Voices of the Holocaust" (www.bl.uk/learning/histcitizen/voices/ho locaust.html). A project of the British Library containing audio testimonies, basic Holocaust information, activities, maps, glossaries, and timelines. Part of the British Library's Sound Archives Oral History Programme.

Yad Vashem: The International School for Holocaust Studies (www1. yadvashem.org/vy/en/education/index.asp). A project of the Holocaust Martyrs' and Heroes' Remembrance Authority of Israel. The site contains extensive video lectures and testimonies, online courses, the Holocaust History Museum, the Art Museum, the Holocaust Resource Center database, and "Children of the Ghetto," an interactive website for children about life in the ghettos.

Index

Picture Credits

Cover: United States Holocaust Memorial Museum
> The views or opinions expressed in this book, and the context in which the image is used, does not necessarily reflect the views or policy of, nor imply approval or endorsement by, the United States Holocaust Memorial Museum.

About the Author

Charles and Linda George have written more than 60 nonfiction books for children and young adults on topics as wide-ranging as the Holocaust, world religions, the Civil Rights Movement, ancient civilizations, extreme sports, and science. They both retired from teaching in Texas public schools to write full time. They live in a small town in West Texas.